MznLnx

Missing Links Exam Preps

Exam Prep for

Marketing Management

Kotler & Keller, 12th Edition

The MznLnx Exam Prep is your link from the texbook and lecture to your exams.
The MznLnx Exam Preps are unauthorized and comprehensive reviews of your textbooks.

All material provided by MznLnx and Rico Publications (c) 2010
Textbook publishers and textbook authors do not particpate in or contribute to these reviews.

MznLnx

Rico Publications

Exam Prep for Marketing Management
12th Edition
Kotler & Keller

Publisher: Raymond Houge
Assistant Editor: Michael Rouger
Text and Cover Designer: Lisa Buckner
Marketing Manager: Sara Swagger
Project Manager, Editorial Production: Jerry Emerson
Art Director: Vernon Lowerui

Product Manager: Dave Mason
Editorial Assitant: Rachel Guzmanji
Pedagogy: Debra Long
Cover Image: Jim Reed/Getty Images
Text and Cover Printer: City Printing, Inc.
Compositor: Media Mix, Inc.

(c) 2010 Rico Publications
ALL RIGHTS RESERVED. No part of this work covered by the copyright may be reproduced or used in any form or by an means--graphic, electronic, or mechanical, including photocopying, recording, taping, Web distribution, information storage, and retrieval systems, or in any other manner--without the written permission of the publisher.

Printed in the United States
ISBN:

For more information about our products, contact us at:
Dave.Mason@RicoPublications.com

For permission to use material from this text or product, submit a request online to:
Dave.Mason@RicoPublications.com

Contents

CHAPTER 1
Defining Marketing for the 21st Century — 1

CHAPTER 2
Developing Marketing Strategies and Plans — 9

CHAPTER 3
Gathering information and Scanning the Environment — 17

CHAPTER 4
Conducting Marketing Research and Forecasting Demand — 22

CHAPTER 5
Creating Customer Value, Satisfaction, and Loyalty — 29

CHAPTER 6
Analyzing Consumer Markets — 36

CHAPTER 7
Analyzing Business Markets — 42

CHAPTER 8
Identifying Market Segments and Targets — 45

CHAPTER 9
Creating Brand Equity — 50

CHAPTER 10
Crafting the Brand Positioning — 55

CHAPTER 11
Dealing with Competition — 59

CHAPTER 12
Setting Product Strategy — 62

CHAPTER 13
Designing and Managing Services — 65

CHAPTER 14
Developing Pricing Strategies and Programs — 69

CHAPTER 15
Designing and Managing Value Networks and Channels — 74

CHAPTER 16
Managing Retailing, Wholesaling, and Logistics — 77

CHAPTER 17
Designing and Managing Integrated Marketing Communications — 81

CHAPTER 18
Managing Mass Communications — 86

CHAPTER 19
Managing Personal Communications — 90

CHAPTER 20
Introducing New Market Offerings — 95

Contents (Cont.)

CHAPTER 21
  Tapping into Global Markets   100
CHAPTER 22
  Managing a Holistic Marketing Organization   104
ANSWER KEY   108

TO THE STUDENT

COMPREHENSIVE

The *MznLnx* Exam Prep series is designed to help you pass your exams. Editors at MznLnx review your textbooks and then prepare these practice exams to help you master the textbook material. Unlike study guides, workbooks, and practice tests provided by the texbook publisher and textbook authors, *MznLnx* gives you **all** of the material in each chapter in exam form, not just samples, so you can be sure to nail your exam.

MECHANICAL

The MznLnx Exam Prep series creates exams that will help you learn the subject matter as well as test you on your understanding. Each question is designed to help you master the concept. Just working through the exams, you gain an understanding of the subject--its a simple mechanical process that produces success.

INTEGRATED STUDY GUIDE AND REVIEW

MznLnx is not just a set of exams designed to test you, its also a comprehensive review of the subject content. Each exam question is also a review of the concept, making sure that you will get the answer correct without having to go to other sources of material. You learn as you go! Its the easiest way to pass an exam.

HUMOR

Studying can be tedious and dry. MznLnx's instructional design includes moderate humor within the exam questions on occassion, to break the tedium and revitalize the brain

Chapter 1. Defining Marketing for the 21st Century

1. _____ is a corporate title referring to an executive responsible for various marketing in an organization. Most often the position reports to the chief executive officer.

With primary or shared responsibility for areas such as sales management, product development, distribution channel management, public relations, marketing communications (including advertising and promotions), pricing, market research, and customer service.

   a. Tudou
   b. MySpace
   c. Direct investment
   d. Chief Marketing Officer

2. _____ is defined by the American _____ Association as the activity, set of institutions, and processes for creating, communicating, delivering, and exchanging offerings that have value for customers, clients, partners, and society at large. The term developed from the original meaning which referred literally to going to market, as in shopping, or going to a market to sell goods or services.

_____ practice tends to be seen as a creative industry, which includes advertising, distribution and selling.

   a. Product naming
   b. Customer acquisition management
   c. Marketing myopia
   d. Marketing

3. _____ is a business discipline which is focused on the practical application of marketing techniques and the management of a firm's marketing resources and activities. Marketing managers are often responsible for influencing the level, timing, and composition of customer demand accepted definition of the term. In part, this is because the role of a marketing manager can vary significantly based on a business' size, corporate culture, and industry context.
   a. Performance-based advertising
   b. Door-to-door
   c. Business structure
   d. Marketing management

4. _____ is a technique used in propaganda and advertising. Also known as association, this is a technique of projecting positive or negative qualities (praise or blame) of a person, entity, object, or value (an individual, group, organization, nation, patriotism, etc.) to another in order to make the second more acceptable or to discredit it.
   a. Sexism,
   b. Micro ads
   c. Supplier
   d. Transfer

5. _____ is an advertisement in which a particular product specifically mentions a competitor by name for the express purpose of showing why the competitor is inferior to the product naming it.

This should not be confused with parody advertisements, where a fictional product is being advertised for the purpose of poking fun at the particular advertisement, nor should it be confused with the use of a coined brand name for the purpose of comparing the product without actually naming an actual competitor. ('Wikipedia tastes better and is less filling than the Encyclopedia Galactica.')

In the 1980s, during what has been referred to as the cola wars, soft-drink manufacturer Pepsi ran a series of advertisements where people, caught on hidden camera, in a blind taste test, chose Pepsi over rival Coca-Cola.

   a. Cost per conversion
   b. GL-70
   c. Heavy-up
   d. Comparative advertising

6. _____ is the practice of individuals including commercial businesses, governments and institutions, facilitating the sale of their products or services to other companies or organizations that in turn resell them, use them as components in products or services they offer _____ is also called business-to-_____ for short. (Note that while marketing to government entities shares some of the same dynamics of organizational marketing, B2G Marketing is meaningfully different.)

   a. Law of disruption   b. Mass marketing
   c. Disruptive technology   d. Business marketing

7. _____ is a broad label that refers to any individuals or households that use goods and services generated within the economy. The concept of a _____ is used in different contexts, so that the usage and significance of the term may vary.

A _____ is a person who uses any product or service.

   a. 6-3-5 Brainwriting   b. Consumer
   c. Power III   d. 180SearchAssistant

8. In economics, _____ is the desire to own something and the ability to pay for it. The term _____ signifies the ability or the willingness to buy a particular commodity at a given point of time .

   a. Demand   b. Discretionary spending
   c. Market system   d. Market dominance

9. A _____ is the space, actual or metaphorical, in which a market operates. The term is also used in a trademark law context to denote the actual consumer environment, ie. the 'real world' in which products and services are provided and consumed.

   a. 180SearchAssistant   b. Power III
   c. 6-3-5 Brainwriting   d. Marketplace

10. _____ - an information and communication based electronic exchange environment - is a relatively new concept in marketing. Since physical boundaries no longer interfere with buy/sell decisions, the world has grown into several industry specific _____s which are integration of marketplaces through sophisticated computer and telecommunication technologies. The term _____ was introduced by Rayport and Sviokla in 1994 (see Rayport, Jeffrey F.

   a. Value chain   b. Market segment
   c. Marketspace   d. Kano model

11. _____ is the study of when, why, how, where and what people do or do not buy products. It blends elements from psychology, sociology, social psychology, anthropology and economics. It attempts to understand the buyer decision making process, both individually and in groups. It studies characteristics of individual consumers such as demographics and behavioural variables in an attempt to understand people's wants. It also tries to assess influences on the consumer from groups such as family, friends, reference groups, and society in general.

   a. Multidimensional scaling   b. Communal marketing
   c. Consumer confidence   d. Consumer behavior

12. _____ is a process by which government's control over businesses and individuals is reduced or eliminated. It is the removal of some governmental controls over a market. _____ does not mean elimination of laws against fraud, but eliminating or reducing government control of how business is done, thereby moving toward a more free market.

   a. Deregulation
   b. Consumer spending
   c. Value added
   d. Power III

13. _____ in its literal sense is the process of transformation of local or regional phenomena into global ones. It can be described as a process by which the people of the world are unified into a single society and function together.

This process is a combination of economic, technological, sociocultural and political forces.

   a. Power III
   b. 180SearchAssistant
   c. Globalization
   d. 6-3-5 Brainwriting

14. _____ is a rivalry between individuals, groups, nations for territory, a niche, or allocation of resources. It arises whenever two or more parties strive for a goal which cannot be shared. _____ occurs naturally between living organisms which co-exist in the same environment.

   a. Price competition
   b. Competition
   c. Non-price competition
   d. Price fixing

15. On an intranet or B2E Enterprise Web portals, personalization is often based on user attributes such as department, functional area, or role. The term _____ in this context refers to the ability of users to modify the page layout or specify what content should be displayed.

There are two categories of personalizations:

1. Rule-based
2. Content-based

Web personalization models include rules-based filtering, based on 'if this, then that' rules processing, and collaborative filtering, which serves relevant material to customers by combining their own personal preferences with the preferences of like-minded others. Collaborative filtering works well for books, music, video, etc.

   a. Self branding
   b. Cashmere Agency
   c. Customization
   d. Movin'

16. An _____ is the manufacturing of a good or service within a category. Although _____ is a broad term for any kind of economic production, in economics and urban planning _____ is a synonym for the secondary sector, which is a type of economic activity involved in the manufacturing of raw materials into goods and products.

There are four key industrial economic sectors: the primary sector, largely raw material extraction industries such as mining and farming; the secondary sector, involving refining, construction, and manufacturing; the tertiary sector, which deals with services (such as law and medicine) and distribution of manufactured goods; and the quaternary sector, a relatively new type of knowledge _____ focusing on technological research, design and development such as computer programming, and biochemistry.

a. ACNielsen
b. ADTECH
c. AMAX
d. Industry

17. In economics, _____ is the removal of intermediaries in a supply chain: 'cutting out the middleman'. Instead of going through traditional distribution channels, which had some type of intermediate (such as a distributor, wholesaler, broker, or agent), companies may now deal with every customer directly, for example via the Internet. One important factor is a drop in the cost of servicing customers directly.

a. Consumer-to-consumer
b. Social shopping
c. Disintermediation
d. Spamvertising

18. A _____ is a plan of action designed to achieve a particular goal.

_____ is different from tactics. In military terms, tactics is concerned with the conduct of an engagement while _____ is concerned with how different engagements are linked.

a. Strategy
b. 6-3-5 Brainwriting
c. Power III
d. 180SearchAssistant

19. _____ in economics refers to metrics and measures of output from production processes, per unit of input. Labor _____, for example, is typically measured as a ratio of output per labor-hour, an input. _____ may be conceived of as a metrics of the technical or engineering efficiency of production.

a. Value engineering
b. Power III
c. 180SearchAssistant
d. Productivity

20. _____ is a form of marketing developed from direct response marketing campaigns conducted in the 1970's and 1980's which emphasizes customer retention and satisfaction, rather than a dominant focus on 'point of sale' transactions.

_____ differs from other forms of marketing in that it recognizes the long term value to the firm of keeping customers, as opposed to direct or 'Intrusion' marketing, which focuses upon acquisition of new clients by targeting majority demographics based upon prospective client lists.

_____ refers to long-term and mutually beneficial arrangement wherein both buyer and seller focus on value enhancement through the certain of more satisfying exchange.This approach attempts to transcend the simple purchase exchange process with customer to make more meaningful and richer contact by providing a more holistic, personalized purchase, and use orn consumption experience to create stronger ties.

a. Global marketing
b. Diversity marketing
c. Guerrilla Marketing
d. Relationship marketing

21. _____ consists of the processes a company uses to track and organize its contacts with its current and prospective customers. _____ software is used to support these processes; information about customers and customer interactions can be entered, stored and accessed by employees in different company departments. Typical _____ goals are to improve services provided to customers, and to use customer contact information for targeted marketing.

a. Product bundling
b. Commercialization
c. Demand generation
d. Customer relationship management

22. _____ , according to The American Marketing Association, is 'a planning process designed to assure that all brand contacts received by a customer or prospect for a product, service, or organization are relevant to that person and consistent over time.' (Marketing Power Dictionary)

_____ is a term used to describe a holistic approach to marketing. It aims to ensure consistency of message and the complementary use of media. The concept includes online and offline marketing channels.

a. Integrated marketing communications
b. AMAX
c. ADTECH
d. ACNielsen

23. _____ is an ongoing process that occurs strictly within a company or organization whereby the functional process aligns, motivates and empowers employees at all management levels to consistently deliver a satisfying customer experience. According to Burkitt and Zealley, 'the challenge for _____ is not only to get the right messages across, but to embed them in such a way that they both change and reinforce employee behaviour'.

a. ACNielsen
b. AMAX
c. ADTECH
d. Internal marketing

24. _____ refers to marketing strategies applied directly to a specific consumer.

Having the knowledge on the consumer preferences, there are suggested personalized products and promotions to each consumer.

The _____ is based in four main steps in order to fulfill its goals: Those stages are identify, differentiate, interact, and customize.

a. ADTECH
b. ACNielsen
c. AMAX
d. One-to-one marketing

25. Customer _____ consists of the processes a company uses to track and organize its contacts with its current and prospective customers. CRelationship management software is used to support these processes; information about customers and customer interactions can be entered, stored and accessed by employees in different company departments. Typical CRelationship management goals are to improve services provided to customers, and to use customer contact information for targeted marketing.

a. Marketing
b. Product bundling
c. Relationship management
d. Green marketing

26. The _____ is generally accepted as the use and specification of the four p's describing the strategic position of a product in the marketplace. One version of the origins of the _____ starts in 1948 when James Culliton said that a marketing decision should be a result of something similar to a recipe. This version continued in 1953 when Neil Borden, in his American Marketing Association presidential address, took the recipe idea one step further and coined the term 'Marketing-Mix'.

Chapter 1. Defining Marketing for the 21st Century

- a. 180SearchAssistant
- b. Marketing mix
- c. Power III
- d. 6-3-5 Brainwriting

27. _____ refers to a type of marketing involving the cooperative efforts of a 'for profit' business and a non-profit organization for mutual benefit. The term is sometimes used more broadly and generally to refer to any type of marketing effort for social and other charitable causes, including in-house marketing efforts by non-profit organizations. Cause marketing differs from corporate giving (philanthropy) as the latter generally involves a specific donation that is tax deductible, while cause marketing is a marketing relationship generally not based on a donation.
    - a. Global marketing
    - b. Cause-related marketing
    - c. Digital marketing
    - d. Diversity marketing

28. The _____ concept is an enlightened marketing concept that holds that a company should make good marketing decisions by considering consumers' wants, the company's requirements, and society's long-term interests. It is closely linked with the principles of corporate social responsibility and of sustainable development.

    The concept has an emphasis on social responsibility and suggests that for a company to only focus on exchange relationship with customers might not be suitable in order to sustain long term success.

    - a. Customer franchise
    - b. Societal marketing
    - c. Marketing
    - d. Business-to-business

29. _____ is the systematic application of marketing along with other concepts and techniques to achieve specific behavioral goals for a social good. _____ can be applied to promote, for example, merit goods, make the society avoid demerit goods and thus to promote that considers society's well being as a whole. This may include asking people not to smoke in public areas, for example, ask them to use seat belts, prompting to make them follow speed limits.
    - a. Social marketing
    - b. Market development
    - c. Marketing strategy
    - d. Psychographic

30. In marketing, _____ has come to mean the process by which marketers try to create an image or identity in the minds of their target market for its product, brand, or organization. It is the 'relative competitive comparison' their product occupies in a given market as perceived by the target market.

    Re-_____ involves changing the identity of a product, relative to the identity of competing products, in the collective minds of the target market.

    - a. Moratorium
    - b. Positioning
    - c. GE matrix
    - d. Containerization

31. _____ is a business term meaning the market segment to which a particular good or service is marketed. It is mainly defined by age, gender, geography, socio-economic grouping, technographic, or any other combination of demographics. It is generally studied and mapped by an organization through lists and reports containing demographic information that may have an effect on the marketing of key products or services.
    - a. Distribution
    - b. Brando
    - c. Market specialization
    - d. Category Development Index

32. A _____ is a collection of symbols, experiences and associations connected with a product, a service, a person or any other artifact or entity.

_____s have become increasingly important components of culture and the economy, now being described as 'cultural accessories and personal philosophies'.

Some people distinguish the psychological aspect of a _____ from the experiential aspect.

  a. Brand equity
  b. Brandable software
  c. Store brand
  d. Brand

33. A personal and cultural _____ is a relative ethic _____, an assumption upon which implementation can be extrapolated. A _____ system is a set of consistent _____s and measures that is soo not true. A principle _____ is a foundation upon which other _____s and measures of integrity are based.
  a. Package-on-Package
  b. Supreme Court of the United States
  c. Perceptual maps
  d. Value

34. _____ is one of the four elements of marketing mix. An organization or set of organizations (go-betweens) involved in the process of making a product or service available for use or consumption by a consumer or business user.

The other three parts of the marketing mix are product, pricing, and promotion.

  a. Japan Advertising Photographers' Association
  b. Better Living Through Chemistry
  c. Distribution
  d. Comparison-Shopping agent

35. The _____ is a marketing term and refers to all of the forces outside of marketing that affect marketing management's ability to build and maintain successful relationships with target customers. The _____ consists of both the macroenvironment and the microenvironment.

The microenvironment refers to the forces that are close to the company and affect its ability to serve its customers.

  a. Customer franchise
  b. Business-to-consumer
  c. Psychographic
  d. Market environment

36. A _____ or logistics network is the system of organizations, people, technology, activities, information and resources involved in moving a product or service from supplier to customer. _____ activities transform natural resources, raw materials and components into a finished product that is delivered to the end customer. In sophisticated _____ systems, used products may re-enter the _____ at any point where residual value is recyclable.
  a. Purchasing
  b. Demand chain management
  c. Supply chain network
  d. Supply chain

37. A _____ is a process that can allow an organization to concentrate its limited resources on the greatest opportunities to increase sales and achieve a sustainable competitive advantage. A _____ should be centered around the key concept that customer satisfaction is the main goal.

A _____ is most effective when it is an integral component of corporate strategy, defining how the organization will successfully engage customers, prospects, and competitors in the market arena.

a. Societal marketing
c. Psychographic
b. Marketing strategy
d. Cyberdoc

38. _____ in organizations and public policy is both the organizational process of creating and maintaining a plan; and the psychological process of thinking about the activities required to create a desired goal on some scale. As such, it is a fundamental property of intelligent behavior. This thought process is essential to the creation and refinement of a plan, or integration of it with other plans, that is, it combines forecasting of developments with the preparation of scenarios of how to react to them.

a. 180SearchAssistant
c. 6-3-5 Brainwriting
b. Planning
d. Power III

Chapter 2. Developing Marketing Strategies and Plans

1. _____ is defined by the American _____ Association as the activity, set of institutions, and processes for creating, communicating, delivering, and exchanging offerings that have value for customers, clients, partners, and society at large. The term developed from the original meaning which referred literally to going to market, as in shopping, or going to a market to sell goods or services.

_____ practice tends to be seen as a creative industry, which includes advertising, distribution and selling.

   a. Customer acquisition management
   b. Marketing myopia
   c. Product naming
   d. Marketing

2. A personal and cultural _____ is a relative ethic _____, an assumption upon which implementation can be extrapolated. A _____ system is a set of consistent _____s and measures that is soo not true. A principle _____ is a foundation upon which other _____s and measures of integrity are based.
   a. Perceptual maps
   b. Package-on-Package
   c. Supreme Court of the United States
   d. Value

3. In marketing, _____ has come to mean the process by which marketers try to create an image or identity in the minds of their target market for its product, brand, or organization. It is the 'relative competitive comparison' their product occupies in a given market as perceived by the target market.

Re-_____ involves changing the identity of a product, relative to the identity of competing products, in the collective minds of the target market.

   a. GE matrix
   b. Moratorium
   c. Positioning
   d. Containerization

4. _____ refers to a business or organization attempting to acquire goods or services to accomplish the goals of the enterprise. Though there are several organizations that attempt to set standards in the _____ process, processes can vary greatly between organizations. Typically the word '_____' is not used interchangeably with the word 'procurement', since procurement typically includes Expediting, Supplier Quality, and Traffic and Logistics (T'L) in addition to _____.
   a. Supply network
   b. Purchasing
   c. Supply chain
   d. Drop shipping

5. The _____ is a concept from business management that was first described and popularized by Michael Porter in his 1985 best-seller, Competitive Advantage: Creating and Sustaining Superior Performance.

A _____ is a chain of activities. Products pass through all activities of the chain in order and at each activity the product gains some value.

   a. Mass marketing
   b. Relationship management
   c. Value chain
   d. Business-to-business

6. A _____ is a complex set of social and technical resources. _____s work together via relationships to create social goods (public goods) or economic value.

This value takes the form of knowledge and other intangibles and/or financial value.

a. 180SearchAssistant
b. Value network
c. 6-3-5 Brainwriting
d. Power III

7. In the field of marketing, a customer _____ consists of the sum total of benefits which a vendor promises that a customer will receive in return for the customer's associated payment (or other value-transfer.)

Put simply, the _____ is what the customer gets for his money.

Accordingly, a customer can evaluate a company's value-proposition on two broad dimensions with multiple subsets:

1. relative performance: what the customer gets from the vendor relative to a competitor's offering;
2. price: which consists of the payment the customer makes to acquire the product or service; plus the access cost

The vendor-company's marketing and sales efforts offer a customer _____; the vendor-company's delivery and customer-service processes then fulfill that value-proposition.

A value-proposition can assist in a firm's marketing strategy, and may guide a business to target a particular market segment.

a. DefCom Australia
b. Relationship management
c. Marketing performance measurement and management
d. Value proposition

8. _____ describes the situation when output from (or information about the result of) an event or phenomenon in the past will influence the same event/phenomenon in the present or future. When an event is part of a chain of cause-and-effect that forms a circuit or loop, then the event is said to 'feed back' into itself.

_____ is also a synonym for:

- _____ Signal; the information about the initial event that is the basis for subsequent modification of the event.
- _____ Loop; the causal path that leads from the initial generation of the _____ signal to the subsequent modification of the event.

_____ is a mechanism, process or signal that is looped back to control a system within itself. Such a loop is called a _____ loop.

a. Feedback
b. Power III
c. 6-3-5 Brainwriting
d. 180SearchAssistant

Chapter 2. Developing Marketing Strategies and Plans

9. Core competency is something that a firm can do well and that meets the following three conditions:

   1. It provides consumer benefits
   2. It is not easy for competitors to imitate
   3. It can be leveraged widely to many products and markets.

A core competency can take various forms, including technical/subject matter know how, a reliable process, and/or close relationships with customers and suppliers (Mascarenhas et al. 1998.) It may also include product development or culture, such as employee dedication.

_____ are particular strengths relative to other organizations in the industry which provide the fundamental basis for the provision of added value.

   a. 180SearchAssistant
   b. Power III
   c. 6-3-5 Brainwriting
   d. Core competencies

10. A _____ or logistics network is the system of organizations, people, technology, activities, information and resources involved in moving a product or service from supplier to customer. _____ activities transform natural resources, raw materials and components into a finished product that is delivered to the end customer. In sophisticated _____ systems, used products may re-enter the _____ at any point where residual value is recyclable.
   a. Supply chain network
   b. Demand chain management
   c. Purchasing
   d. Supply chain

11. Cognition is the scientific term for 'the process of thought.' Its usage varies in different ways in accord with different disciplines: For example, in psychology and _____ science it refers to an information processing view of an individual's psychological functions. Other interpretations of the meaning of cognition link it to the development of concepts; individual minds, groups, organizations, and even larger coalitions of entities, can be modelled as 'societies' (Society of Mind), which cooperate to form concepts.

The autonomous elements of each 'society' would have the opportunity to demonstrate emergent behavior in the face of some crisis or opportunity.

   a. Power III
   b. Cognitive
   c. 6-3-5 Brainwriting
   d. 180SearchAssistant

12. _____ consists of the processes a company uses to track and organize its contacts with its current and prospective customers. _____ software is used to support these processes; information about customers and customer interactions can be entered, stored and accessed by employees in different company departments. Typical _____ goals are to improve services provided to customers, and to use customer contact information for targeted marketing.
   a. Commercialization
   b. Demand generation
   c. Customer relationship management
   d. Product bundling

Chapter 2. Developing Marketing Strategies and Plans

13. _____ is an organization's process of defining its strategy and making decisions on allocating its resources to pursue this strategy, including its capital and people. Various business analysis techniques can be used in _____, including SWOT analysis (Strengths, Weaknesses, Opportunities, and Threats) and PEST analysis (Political, Economic, Social, and Technological analysis) or STEER analysis involving Socio-cultural, Technological, Economic, Ecological, and Regulatory factors and EPISTEL (Environment, Political, Informatic, Social, Technological, Economic and Legal)

_____ is the formal consideration of an organization's future course. All _____ deals with at least one of three key questions:

1. 'What do we do?'
2. 'For whom do we do it?'
3. 'How do we excel?'

In business _____, the third question is better phrased 'How can we beat or avoid competition?'. (Bradford and Duncan, page 1.)

a. 6-3-5 Brainwriting
b. Power III
c. Strategic planning
d. 180SearchAssistant

14. A _____ is a type of business entity in which partners (owners) share with each other the profits or losses of the business undertaking in which all have invested. _____s are often favored over corporations for taxation purposes, as the _____ structure does not generally incur a tax on profits before it is distributed to the partners (i.e. there is no dividend tax levied.) However, depending on the _____ structure and the jurisdiction in which it operates, owners of a _____ may be exposed to greater personal liability than they would as shareholders of a corporation.

a. Partnership
b. Competition law
c. Fair Debt Collection Practices Act
d. Brand piracy

15. _____ in organizations and public policy is both the organizational process of creating and maintaining a plan; and the psychological process of thinking about the activities required to create a desired goal on some scale. As such, it is a fundamental property of intelligent behavior. This thought process is essential to the creation and refinement of a plan, or integration of it with other plans, that is, it combines forecasting of developments with the preparation of scenarios of how to react to them.

a. Planning
b. Power III
c. 6-3-5 Brainwriting
d. 180SearchAssistant

16. Customer _____ consists of the processes a company uses to track and organize its contacts with its current and prospective customers. CRelationship management software is used to support these processes; information about customers and customer interactions can be entered, stored and accessed by employees in different company departments. Typical CRelationship management goals are to improve services provided to customers, and to use customer contact information for targeted marketing.

a. Marketing
b. Product bundling
c. Relationship management
d. Green marketing

17. A _____ is a written document that details the necessary actions to achieve one or more marketing objectives. It can be for a product or service, a brand, or a product line. _____s cover between one and five years.

Chapter 2. Developing Marketing Strategies and Plans

a. Marketing strategy
b. Disruptive technology
c. Prosumer
d. Marketing plan

18. A _____ is a brief statement of the purpose of a company, organization. It is ideally used to guide the actions of the organization.

_____s often contain the following:

- Purpose of the organization
- The organization's primary stakeholders: clients, stockholders, etc.
- Responsibilities of the organization towards these stockholders
- Products and services offered

Generally shorter _____s are more effective than longer ones.

In developing a _____:

- Encourage input as feasible from employees, volunteers, and other stakeholders
- Publicize it broadly

The _____ can be used to resolve differences between business stakeholders. Stakeholders include: employees including managers and executives, stockholders, board of directors, customers, suppliers, distributors, creditors, governments (local, state, federal, etc.), unions, competitors, NGO's, and the general public.

a. Power III
b. Mission statement
c. 6-3-5 Brainwriting
d. 180SearchAssistant

19. _____ is one of the four Ps of the marketing mix. The other three aspects are product, promotion, and place. It is also a key variable in microeconomic price allocation theory.
a. Price
b. Competitor indexing
c. Pricing
d. Relationship based pricing

20. _____ is understood as a business unit within the overall corporate identity which is distinguishable from other business because it serves a defined external market where management can conduct strategic planning in relation to products and markets. When companies become really large, they are best thought of as being composed of a number of businesses (or _____s.)

In the broader domain of strategic management, the phrase '_____' came into use in the 1960s, largely as a result of General Electric's many units.

a. Corporate strategy
b. Cost leadership
c. Strategic business unit
d. Business strategy

Chapter 2. Developing Marketing Strategies and Plans

21. _____ is an idea in the field of Organizational studies and management which describes the psychology, attitudes, experiences, beliefs and Values (personal and cultural values)of an organization. It has been defined as 'the specific collection of values and norms that are shared by people and groups in an organization and that control the way they interact with each other and with stakeholders outside the organization.'

This definition continues to explain organizational values also known as 'beliefs and ideas about what kinds of goals members of an organization should pursue and ideas about the appropriate kinds or standards of behavior organizational members should use to achieve these goals. From organizational values develop organizational norms, guidelines or expectations that prescribe appropriate kinds of behavior by employees in particular situations and control the behavior of organizational members towards one another.'

_____ is not the same as corporate culture.

- a. Organizational culture
- b. ADTECH
- c. Organizational structure
- d. ACNielsen

22. _____ is difficult to define. For example, in 1952, Alfred Kroeber and Clyde Kluckhohn compiled a list of 164 definitions of '_____' in _____: A Critical Review of Concepts and Definitions. However, the word '_____' is most commonly used in three basic senses:

- excellence of taste in the fine arts and humanities
- an integrated pattern of human knowledge, belief, and behavior that depends upon the capacity for symbolic thought and social learning
- the set of shared attitudes, values, goals, and practices that characterizes an institution, organization or group.

When the concept first emerged in eighteenth- and nineteenth-century Europe, it connoted a process of cultivation or improvement, as in agriculture or horticulture. In the nineteenth century, it came to refer first to the betterment or refinement of the individual, especially through education, and then to the fulfillment of national aspirations or ideals.

- a. AStore
- b. Culture
- c. Albert Einstein
- d. African Americans

23. In economics, an externality or spillover of an economic transaction is an impact on a party that is not directly involved in the transaction. In such a case, prices do not reflect the full costs or benefits in production or consumption of a product or service. A positive impact is called an _____ benefit, while a negative impact is called an _____ cost.
- a. ACNielsen
- b. ADTECH
- c. AMAX
- d. External

24. _____ is a strategic planning method used to evaluate the Strengths, Weaknesses, Opportunities, and Threats involved in a project or in a business venture. It involves specifying the objective of the business venture or project and identifying the internal and external factors that are favorable and unfavorable to achieving that objective. The technique is credited to Albert Humphrey, who led a research project at Stanford University in the 1960s and 1970s using data from Fortune 500 companies.

a. Market environment
c. Product differentiation
b. Lead scoring
d. SWOT analysis

25. _____ is a rivalry between individuals, groups, nations for territory, a niche, or allocation of resources. It arises whenever two or more parties strive for a goal which cannot be shared. _____ occurs naturally between living organisms which co-exist in the same environment.
   a. Price competition
   c. Non-price competition
   b. Price fixing
   d. Competition

26. In economics, business, retail, and accounting, a _____ is the value of money that has been used up to produce something, and hence is not available for use anymore. In economics, a _____ is an alternative that is given up as a result of a decision. In business, the _____ may be one of acquisition, in which case the amount of money expended to acquire it is counted as _____.
   a. Variable cost
   c. Transaction cost
   b. Fixed costs
   d. Cost

27. _____ is a concept developed by Michael Porter, used in business strategy. It describes a way to establish the competitive advantage. _____, in basic words, means the lowest cost of operation in the industry.
   a. Chaotics
   c. Cost leadership
   b. Corporate strategy
   d. Strategic group

28. A _____ is a concept used in strategic management that groups companies within an industry that have similar business models or similar combinations of strategies. For example, the restaurant industry can be divided into several _____s including fast-food and fine-dining based on variables such as preparation time, pricing, and presentation. The number of groups within an industry and their composition depends on the dimensions used to define the groups.
   a. Corporate strategy
   c. Strategic business unit
   b. Strategic group
   d. Switching cost

29. _____ is the management of the flow of goods, information and other resources, including energy and people, between the point of origin and the point of consumption in order to meet the requirements of consumers (frequently, and originally, military organizations.) _____ involves the integration of information, transportation, inventory, warehousing, material-handling, and packaging. _____ is a channel of the supply chain which adds the value of time and place utility.
   a. 180SearchAssistant
   c. Power III
   b. 6-3-5 Brainwriting
   d. Logistics

30. _____ is an advertisement in which a particular product specifically mentions a competitor by name for the express purpose of showing why the competitor is inferior to the product naming it.

This should not be confused with parody advertisements, where a fictional product is being advertised for the purpose of poking fun at the particular advertisement, nor should it be confused with the use of a coined brand name for the purpose of comparing the product without actually naming an actual competitor. ('Wikipedia tastes better and is less filling than the Encyclopedia Galactica.')

In the 1980s, during what has been referred to as the cola wars, soft-drink manufacturer Pepsi ran a series of advertisements where people, caught on hidden camera, in a blind taste test, chose Pepsi over rival Coca-Cola.

Chapter 2. Developing Marketing Strategies and Plans

a. Heavy-up
b. GL-70
c. Cost per conversion
d. Comparative advertising

31. _____ is a recursive process where two or more people or organizations work together toward an intersection of common goals -- for example, an intellectual endeavor that is creative in nature--by sharing knowledge, learning and building consensus. _____ does not require leadership and can sometimes bring better results through decentralization and egalitarianism. In particular, teams that work collaboratively can obtain greater resources, recognition and reward when facing competition for finite resources. _____ is also present in opposing goals exhibiting the notion of adversarial _____, though this notion is atypical of the annotation that people have given towards their understanding of _____.

a. Power III
b. 180SearchAssistant
c. 6-3-5 Brainwriting
d. Collaboration

32. _____ is the realization of an application idea, model, design, specification, standard, algorithm an _____ is a realization of a technical specification or algorithm as a program, software component, or other computer system. Many _____s may exist for a given specification or standard.

a. ADTECH
b. ACNielsen
c. AMAX
d. Implementation

33. _____ is the ongoing process of identifying and articulating market requirements that define a product's feature set.

a. Targeted advertising
b. Brand parity
c. Market intelligence
d. Product planning

Chapter 3. Gathering information and Scanning the Environment

1. _____ is defined by the American _____ Association as the activity, set of institutions, and processes for creating, communicating, delivering, and exchanging offerings that have value for customers, clients, partners, and society at large. The term developed from the original meaning which referred literally to going to market, as in shopping, or going to a market to sell goods or services.

_____ practice tends to be seen as a creative industry, which includes advertising, distribution and selling.

  a. Customer acquisition management
  b. Marketing
  c. Product naming
  d. Marketing myopia

2. _____ , according to Cornish, 'the process of acquiring and analyzing information in order to understand the market (both existing and potential customers); to determine the current and future needs and preferences, attitudes and behavior of the market; and to assess changes in the business environment that may affect the size and nature of the market in the future.' ('Product', 1997, p147.)

This figure shows how the interaction between variables from producers, communication channels, and consumers vary the effectiveness of _____ which affects the performance of the sales of a new product. The product is central in a circle because it helps to direct what information is gathered and how.

  a. Market intelligence
  b. Brand parity
  c. Line extension
  d. Co-branding

3. _____ refer to a collection of facts usually collected as the result of experience, observation or experiment or a set of premises. This may consist of numbers, words particularly as measurements or observations of a set of variables. _____ are often viewed as a lowest level of abstraction from which information and knowledge are derived.
  a. Sample size
  b. Mean
  c. Pearson product-moment correlation coefficient
  d. Data

4. _____ is the process of extracting hidden patterns from data. As more data is gathered, with the amount of data doubling every three years, _____ is becoming an increasingly important tool to transform this data into information. It is commonly used in a wide range of profiling practices, such as marketing, surveillance, fraud detection and scientific discovery.
  a. Power III
  b. 180SearchAssistant
  c. Structure mining
  d. Data mining

5. A _____ is a structured collection of records or data that is stored in a computer system. The structure is achieved by organizing the data according to a _____ model. The model in most common use today is the relational model.
  a. 180SearchAssistant
  b. Database
  c. Power III
  d. 6-3-5 Brainwriting

6. _____ describes the situation when output from (or information about the result of) an event or phenomenon in the past will influence the same event/phenomenon in the present or future. When an event is part of a chain of cause-and-effect that forms a circuit or loop, then the event is said to 'feed back' into itself.

Chapter 3. Gathering information and Scanning the Environment

_____ is also a synonym for:

- _____ Signal; the information about the initial event that is the basis for subsequent modification of the event.
- _____ Loop; the causal path that leads from the initial generation of the _____ signal to the subsequent modification of the event.

_____ is a mechanism, process or signal that is looped back to control a system within itself. Such a loop is called a _____ loop.

   a. Power III   b. 180SearchAssistant
   c. 6-3-5 Brainwriting   d. Feedback

7. A craze is a product, idea, cultural movement, or model that gains popularity among a small section of the populace then quickly migrates to the mainstream. Crazes are characterized by their lightning fast adoption and swift departure from public awareness. Crazes and _____s are also characterized by their unusually high interest and sales figures relative to the time they are active in the marketplace, as compared with other similar products, ideas, cultural movements or models.
   a. 180SearchAssistant   b. Fad
   c. Power III   d. 6-3-5 Brainwriting

8. _____ or _____ data refers to selected population characteristics as used in government, marketing or opinion research, or the _____ profiles used in such research. Note the distinction from the term 'demography' Commonly-used _____ include race, age, income, disabilities, mobility (in terms of travel time to work or number of vehicles available), educational attainment, home ownership, employment status, and even location.
   a. Albert Einstein   b. AStore
   c. Demographic   d. African Americans

9. _____ is the change in population over time, and can be quantified as the change in the number of individuals in a population using 'per unit time' for measurement. The term _____ can technically refer to any species, but almost always refers to humans, and it is often used informally for the more specific demographic term _____ rate , and is often used to refer specifically to the growth of the population of the world.

Simple models of _____ include the Malthusian Growth Model and the logistic model.

   a. Power III   b. 180SearchAssistant
   c. 6-3-5 Brainwriting   d. Population growth

10. _____ is a term used to describe a person who was born during the demographic Post-World War II baby boom. Many analysts now believe that two distinct cultural generations were born during this baby boom; the older generation is often called the Baby Boom Generation and the younger generation is often called Generation Jones. The term '_____' is sometimes used in a cultural context, and sometimes used to describe someone who was born during the post-WWII baby boom.

a. Greatest Generation   b. Generation X
c. AStore   d. Baby boomer

11. _____s is the social science that studies the production, distribution, and consumption of goods and services. The term _____s comes from the Ancient Greek oá¼°κονομῖα from oá¼¶κος (oikos, 'house') + vÏŒµος (nomos, 'custom' or 'law'), hence 'rules of the house(hold)'. Current _____ models developed out of the broader field of political economy in the late 19th century, owing to a desire to use an empirical approach more akin to the physical sciences.
  a. Economic   b. ADTECH
  c. Industrial organization   d. ACNielsen

12. In economics, _____ is how a nation's total economy is distributed among its population. ._____ has always been a central concern of economic theory and economic policy. Classical economists such as Adam Smith, Thomas Malthus and David Ricardo were mainly concerned with factor _____, that is, the distribution of income between the main factors of production, land, labour and capital.
  a. Inflation rate   b. ACNielsen
  c. Internality   d. Income distribution

13. _____ is one of the four elements of marketing mix. An organization or set of organizations (go-betweens) involved in the process of making a product or service available for use or consumption by a consumer or business user.

The other three parts of the marketing mix are product, pricing, and promotion.

  a. Better Living Through Chemistry   b. Distribution
  c. Japan Advertising Photographers' Association   d. Comparison-Shopping agent

14. _____ is subcontracting a process, such as product design or manufacturing, to a third-party company. The decision to outsource is often made in the interest of lowering cost or making better use of time and energy costs, redirecting or conserving energy directed at the competencies of a particular business, or to make more efficient use of land, labor, capital, (information) technology and resources. _____ became part of the business lexicon during the 1980s.
  a. Outsourcing   b. Intangible assets
  c. ACNielsen   d. In-house

15. In sociology, anthropology and cultural studies, a _____ is a group of people with a culture (whether distinct or hidden) which differentiates them from the larger culture to which they belong. If a particular _____ is characterized by a systematic opposition to the dominant culture, it may be described as a counterculture. As Ken Gelder notes, _____s are social, with their own shared conventions, values and rituals, but they can also seem 'immersed' or self-absorbed--another feature that distinguishes them from countercultures.
  a. 180SearchAssistant   b. Subculture
  c. Power III   d. 6-3-5 Brainwriting

16. Human beings are also considered to be _____ because they have the ability to change raw materials into valuable _____. The term Human _____ can also be defined as the skills, energies, talents, abilities and knowledge that are used for the production of goods or the rendering of services. While taking into account human beings as _____, the following things have to be kept in mind:

- The size of the population
- The capabilities of the individuals in that population

Many _____ cannot be consumed in their original form. They have to be processed in order to change them into more usable commodities.

a. 180SearchAssistant
b. 6-3-5 Brainwriting
c. Power III
d. Resources

17. According to the American Marketing Association, _____ is the marketing of products that are presumed to be environmentally safe. Thus _____ incorporates a broad range of activities, including product modification, changes to the production process, packaging changes, as well as modifying advertising. Yet defining _____ is not a simple task where several meanings intersect and contradict each other; an example of this will be the existence of varying social, environmental and retail definitions attached to this term.

a. Customer Interaction Tracker
b. Commercialization
c. Green marketing
d. Value proposition

18. The phrase _____, according to the Organization for Economic Co-operation and Development, refers to 'creative work undertaken on a systematic basis in order to increase the stock of knowledge, including knowledge of man, culture and society, and the use of this stock of knowledge to devise new applications [sic]' Though it is questionable that an organization is needed for this definition, as it is quite obvious that _____ refers to the _____ of something.

New product design and development is more often than not a crucial factor in the survival of a company. In an industry that is fast changing, firms must continually revise their design and range of products.

a. Power III
b. 180SearchAssistant
c. Research and development
d. 6-3-5 Brainwriting

19. _____ is a technology which allows a user to interact with a computer-simulated environment, whether that environment is a simulation of the real world or an imaginary world. Most current _____ environments are primarily visual experiences, displayed either on a computer screen or through special or stereoscopic displays, but some simulations include additional sensory information, such as sound through speakers or headphones. Some advanced, haptic systems now include tactile information, generally known as force feedback, in medical and gaming applications.

a. 180SearchAssistant
b. 6-3-5 Brainwriting
c. Power III
d. Virtual reality

20. In the United States , a _____ is the name commonly given to a private group, regardless of size, organized to elect political candidates. Legally, what constitutes a '_____' for purposes of regulation is a matter of state and federal law. Under the Federal Election Campaign Act, an organization becomes a 'political committee' by receiving contributions or making expenditures in excess of $1,000 for the purpose of influencing a federal election.

a. Political action committee
b. 6-3-5 Brainwriting
c. Power III
d. 180SearchAssistant

Chapter 4. Conducting Marketing Research and Forecasting Demand

1. _____ is defined by the American _____ Association as the activity, set of institutions, and processes for creating, communicating, delivering, and exchanging offerings that have value for customers, clients, partners, and society at large. The term developed from the original meaning which referred literally to going to market, as in shopping, or going to a market to sell goods or services.

_____ practice tends to be seen as a creative industry, which includes advertising, distribution and selling.

   a. Marketing myopia   b. Product naming
   c. Customer acquisition management   d. Marketing

2. Consumer market research is a form of applied sociology that concentrates on understanding the behaviours, whims and preferences, of consumers in a market-based economy, and aims to understand the effects and comparative success of marketing campaigns. The field of consumer _____ as a statistical science was pioneered by Arthur Nielsen with the founding of the ACNielsen Company in 1923.

Thus _____ is the systematic and objective identification, collection, analysis, and dissemination of information for the purpose of assisting management in decision making related to the identification and solution of problems and opportunities in marketing.

   a. Focus group   b. Marketing research process
   c. Logit analysis   d. Marketing research

3. _____ is a measure of the strength of a brand, product, service relative to competitive offerings. There is often a geographic element to the competitive landscape. In defining _____, you must see to what extent a product, brand, or firm controls a product category in a given geographic area.

   a. Market dominance   b. Market system
   c. Productivity   d. Discretionary spending

4. _____ refer to a collection of facts usually collected as the result of experience, observation or experiment or a set of premises. This may consist of numbers, words particularly as measurements or observations of a set of variables. _____ are often viewed as a lowest level of abstraction from which information and knowledge are derived.

   a. Data   b. Pearson product-moment correlation coefficient
   c. Mean   d. Sample size

5. _____ is a term for unprocessed data, it is also known as primary data. It is a relative term _____ can be input to a computer program or used in manual analysis procedures such as gathering statistics from a survey.

   a. Chief marketing officer   b. Shoppers Food ' Pharmacy
   c. Raw data   d. Product manager

6. Combining Existing _____ Sources with New Primary Data Sources

Imagine that we could get hold of a good collection of surveys taken in earlier years, such as detailed studies about changes going on in this phase and hopefully additional studies in the years to come. Analyzing this data base over time could give us a good picture of what changes actually have taken place in the orientation of the population and of the extent to which new technical concepts did have an impact on subgroups of the population. Furthermore, data archives can help to prepare studies on change over time by monitoring what questions have been asked in earlier years and alerting principal investigators to important questions which should be repeated in planned research projects.

- a. Secondary data
- b. 180SearchAssistant
- c. 6-3-5 Brainwriting
- d. Power III

7. In environmental modeling and especially in hydrology, a _____ model means a model that is acceptably consistent with observed natural processes, i.e. that simulates well, for example, observed river discharge. It is a key concept of the so-called Generalized Likelihood Uncertainty Estimation (GLUE) methodology to quantify how uncertain environmental predictions are.

- a. Behavioral
- b. 6-3-5 Brainwriting
- c. 180SearchAssistant
- d. Power III

8. A _____ is a form of qualitative research in which a group of people are asked about their attitude towards a product, service, concept, advertisement, idea, or packaging. Questions are asked in an interactive group setting where participants are free to talk with other group members.

Ernest Dichter originated the idea of having a 'group therapy' for products and this process is what became known as a _____.

- a. Logit analysis
- b. Cross tabulation
- c. Marketing research process
- d. Focus group

9. In marketing and the social sciences, _____ is a social research technique that involves the direct observation of phenomena in their natural setting. This differentiates it from experimental research in which a quasi-artificial environment is created to control for spurious factors, and where at least one of the variables is manipulated as part of the experiment.

Compared with quantitative research and experimental research, _____ tends to be less reliable but often more valid.

- a. ADTECH
- b. ACNielsen
- c. AMAX
- d. Observational research

10. _____ is a broad label that refers to any individuals or households that use goods and services generated within the economy. The concept of a _____ is used in different contexts, so that the usage and significance of the term may vary.

A _____ is a person who uses any product or service.

a. Power III
b. Consumer
c. 6-3-5 Brainwriting
d. 180SearchAssistant

11. _____ is a field of inquiry that crosscuts disciplines and subject matters . _____ers aim to gather an in-depth understanding of human behavior and the reasons that govern such behavior. The discipline investigates the why and how of decision making, not just what, where, when.
   a. 6-3-5 Brainwriting
   b. 180SearchAssistant
   c. Power III
   d. Qualitative research

12. A _____ is a research instrument consisting of a series of questions and other prompts for the purpose of gathering information from respondents. Although they are often designed for statistical analysis of the responses, this is not always the case. The _____ was invented by Sir Francis Galton.
   a. Questionnaire
   b. Market research
   c. Mystery shoppers
   d. Mystery shopping

13. A _____ is a collection of symbols, experiences and associations connected with a product, a service, a person or any other artifact or entity.

_____s have become increasingly important components of culture and the economy, now being described as 'cultural accessories and personal philosophies'.

Some people distinguish the psychological aspect of a _____ from the experiential aspect.

   a. Brand equity
   b. Brandable software
   c. Store brand
   d. Brand

14. _____ is an investment technique that requires investors to purchase multiple financial products with different maturity dates.

_____ avoids the risk of reinvesting a big portion of assets in an unfavorable financial environment. For example, a person has both a 2015 matured CD and a 2018 matured CD.

   a. Laddering
   b. 6-3-5 Brainwriting
   c. Power III
   d. 180SearchAssistant

15. _____ is the conveying of events in words, images, and sounds often by improvisation or embellishment. Stories or narratives have been shared in every culture and in every land as a means of entertainment, education, preservation of culture and in order to instill moral values. Crucial elements of stories and _____ include plot and characters, as well as the narrative point of view.
   a. 6-3-5 Brainwriting
   b. Storytelling
   c. Power III
   d. 180SearchAssistant

16. _____ is a common word game involving an exchange of words that are associated together.

Once an original word has been chosen, usually randomly or arbitrarily, a player will find a word that they associate with it and make it known to all the players, usually by saying it aloud or writing it down as the next item on a list of words so far used. The next player must then do the same with this previous word.

- a. 180SearchAssistant
- b. 6-3-5 Brainwriting
- c. Power III
- d. Word association

17. _____ is that part of statistical practice concerned with the selection of individual observations intended to yield some knowledge about a population of concern, especially for the purposes of statistical inference. Each observation measures one or more properties (weight, location, etc.) of an observable entity enumerated to distinguish objects or individuals.
- a. Richard Buckminster 'Bucky' Fuller
- b. Sports Marketing Group
- c. AStore
- d. Sampling

18. _____ is the study of when, why, how, where and what people do or do not buy products. It blends elements from psychology, sociology, social psychology, anthropology and economics. It attempts to understand the buyer decision making process, both individually and in groups. It studies characteristics of individual consumers such as demographics and behavioural variables in an attempt to understand people's wants. It also tries to assess influences on the consumer from groups such as family, friends, reference groups, and society in general.
- a. Consumer confidence
- b. Consumer behavior
- c. Communal marketing
- d. Multidimensional scaling

19. _____ in economics refers to metrics and measures of output from production processes, per unit of input. Labor _____, for example, is typically measured as a ratio of output per labor-hour, an input. _____ may be conceived of as a metrics of the technical or engineering efficiency of production.
- a. 180SearchAssistant
- b. Productivity
- c. Value engineering
- d. Power III

20. _____, or Value optimized pricing is a business strategy. It sets selling prices on the perceived value to the customer, rather than on the actual cost of the product, the market price, competitors prices, or the historical price.

The goal of _____ is to align price with value delivered.

- a. Value-based pricing
- b. Jobbing house
- c. Money back guarantee
- d. Service-profit chain

21. _____, in strategic management and marketing, is the percentage or proportion of the total available market or market segment that is being serviced by a company. It can be expressed as a company's sales revenue (from that market) divided by the total sales revenue available in that market. It can also be expressed as a company's unit sales volume (in a market) divided by the total volume of units sold in that market.
- a. Market share
- b. Cyberdoc
- c. Customer relationship management
- d. Demand generation

22. The _____ in statistical process control is a tool used to determine whether a manufacturing or business process is in a state of statistical control or not.

If the chart indicates that the process is currently under control then it can be used with confidence to predict the future performance of the process. If the chart indicates that the process being monitored is not in control, the pattern it reveals can help determine the source of variation to be eliminated to bring the process back into control.

a. Control chart
b. Probability sampling
c. Statistics
d. Survey research

23. The loyalty business model is a business model used in strategic management in which company resources are employed so as to increase the loyalty of customers and other stakeholders in the expectation that corporate objectives will be met or surpassed. A typical example of this type of model is: quality of product or service leads to customer satisfaction, which leads to _____, which leads to profitability.

Fredrick Reichheld (1996) expanded the loyalty business model beyond customers and employees.

a. Customer loyalty
b. 180SearchAssistant
c. Power III
d. 6-3-5 Brainwriting

24. _____ in economics and business is the result of an exchange and from that trade we assign a numerical monetary value to a good, service or asset. If I trade 4 apples for an orange, the _____ of an orange is 4 - apples. Inversely, the _____ of an apple is 1/4 oranges.

a. Price
b. Contribution margin-based pricing
c. Discounts and allowances
d. Pricing

25. In finance, _____ rate of profit or sometimes just return, is the ratio of money gained or lost on an investment relative to the amount of money invested. The amount of money gained or lost may be referred to as interest, profit/loss, gain/loss, or net income/loss. The money invested may be referred to as the asset, capital, principal, or the cost basis of the investment.

a. Power III
b. 6-3-5 Brainwriting
c. 180SearchAssistant
d. Rate of return

26. In accounting, _____ has a very specific meaning. It is an outflow of cash or other valuable assets from a person or company to another person or company. This outflow of cash is generally one side of a trade for products or services that have equal or better current or future value to the buyer than to the seller.

a. ADTECH
b. AMAX
c. ACNielsen
d. Expense

27. In economics, business, retail, and accounting, a _____ is the value of money that has been used up to produce something, and hence is not available for use anymore. In economics, a _____ is an alternative that is given up as a result of a decision. In business, the _____ may be one of acquisition, in which case the amount of money expended to acquire it is counted as _____.

a. Variable cost
b. Transaction cost
c. Fixed costs
d. Cost

Chapter 4. Conducting Marketing Research and Forecasting Demand

28. In economics, _____ is the desire to own something and the ability to pay for it. The term _____ signifies the ability or the willingness to buy a particular commodity at a given point of time .

  a. Discretionary spending
  b. Market dominance
  c. Market system
  d. Demand

29. _____ is the process of estimation in unknown situations. Prediction is a similar, but more general term. Both can refer to estimation of time series, cross-sectional or longitudinal data.
  a. Power III
  b. 180SearchAssistant
  c. 6-3-5 Brainwriting
  d. Forecasting

30. _____ is one of the four growth strategies of the Product-Market Growth Matrix defined by Ansoff. _____ occurs when a company enters/penetrates a market with current products. The best way to achieve this is by gaining competitors' customers (part of their market share.)
  a. Marketization
  b. Market penetration
  c. Horizontal market
  d. Pasar pagi

31. _____ generally refers to a list of all planned expenses and revenues. It is a plan for saving and spending. A _____ is an important concept in microeconomics, which uses a _____ line to illustrate the trade-offs between two or more goods.
  a. 180SearchAssistant
  b. 6-3-5 Brainwriting
  c. Power III
  d. Budget

32. A _____ is a plan of action designed to achieve a particular goal.

_____ is different from tactics. In military terms, tactics is concerned with the conduct of an engagement while _____ is concerned with how different engagements are linked.

  a. 6-3-5 Brainwriting
  b. Power III
  c. 180SearchAssistant
  d. Strategy

33. An _____ is the manufacturing of a good or service within a category. Although _____ is a broad term for any kind of economic production, in economics and urban planning _____ is a synonym for the secondary sector, which is a type of economic activity involved in the manufacturing of raw materials into goods and products.

There are four key industrial economic sectors: the primary sector, largely raw material extraction industries such as mining and farming; the secondary sector, involving refining, construction, and manufacturing; the tertiary sector, which deals with services (such as law and medicine) and distribution of manufactured goods; and the quaternary sector, a relatively new type of knowledge _____ focusing on technological research, design and development such as computer programming, and biochemistry.

  a. ADTECH
  b. ACNielsen
  c. AMAX
  d. Industry

34. _____ is a way of expressing knowledge or belief that an event will occur or has occurred. In mathematics the concept has been given an exact meaning in _____ theory, that is used extensively in such areas of study as mathematics, statistics, finance, gambling, science, and philosophy to draw conclusions about the likelihood of potential events and the underlying mechanics of complex systems.

   a. Heteroskedastic   b. Data

   c. Probability   d. Linear regression

35. The _____ is a systematic, interactive forecasting method which relies on a panel of independent experts. The carefully selected experts answer questionnaires in two or more rounds. After each round, a facilitator provides an anonymous summary of the experts' forecasts from the previous round as well as the reasons they provided for their judgments.

   a. Delphi method   b. Power III

   c. 180SearchAssistant   d. Futurist

36. In statistics, _____ is a technique that can be applied to time series data, either to produce smoothed data for presentation, or to make forecasts. The time series data themselves are a sequence of observations. The observed phenomenon may be an essentially random process, or it may be an orderly, but noisy, process.

   a. ACNielsen   b. Exponential smoothing

   c. ADTECH   d. AMAX

37. In statistics and image processing, to smooth a data set is to create an approximating function that attempts to capture important patterns in the data, while leaving out noise or other fine-scale structures/rapid phenomena. Many different algorithms are used in _____. One of the most common algorithms is the 'moving average', often used to try to capture important trends in repeated statistical surveys.

   a. Power III   b. 6-3-5 Brainwriting

   c. Smoothing   d. 180SearchAssistant

Chapter 5. Creating Customer Value, Satisfaction, and Loyalty

1. A personal and cultural _____ is a relative ethic _____, an assumption upon which implementation can be extrapolated. A _____ system is a set of consistent _____s and measures that is soo not true. A principle _____ is a foundation upon which other _____s and measures of integrity are based.
   a. Supreme Court of the United States
   b. Value
   c. Package-on-Package
   d. Perceptual maps

2. In economics, business, retail, and accounting, a _____ is the value of money that has been used up to produce something, and hence is not available for use anymore. In economics, a _____ is an alternative that is given up as a result of a decision. In business, the _____ may be one of acquisition, in which case the amount of money expended to acquire it is counted as _____.
   a. Transaction cost
   b. Variable cost
   c. Fixed costs
   d. Cost

3. In the field of marketing, a customer _____ consists of the sum total of benefits which a vendor promises that a customer will receive in return for the customer's associated payment (or other value-transfer.)

   Put simply, the _____ is what the customer gets for his money.

   Accordingly, a customer can evaluate a company's value-proposition on two broad dimensions with multiple subsets:

   1. relative performance: what the customer gets from the vendor relative to a competitor's offering;
   2. price: which consists of the payment the customer makes to acquire the product or service; plus the access cost

   The vendor-company's marketing and sales efforts offer a customer _____; the vendor-company's delivery and customer-service processes then fulfill that value-proposition.

   A value-proposition can assist in a firm's marketing strategy, and may guide a business to target a particular market segment.

   a. Relationship management
   b. Value proposition
   c. Marketing performance measurement and management
   d. DefCom Australia

4. _____, a business term, is a measure of how products and services supplied by a company meet or surpass customer expectation. It is seen as a key performance indicator within business and is part of the four perspectives of a Balanced Scorecard.

   In a competitive marketplace where businesses compete for customers, _____ is seen as a key differentiator and increasingly has become a key element of business strategy.

   a. Customer satisfaction
   b. Psychological pricing
   c. Supplier diversity
   d. Customer base

5. The _____ is an economic indicator that measures the satisfaction of consumers across the U.S. economy. It is produced by the National Quality Research Center (NQRC) at the University of Michigan in Ann Arbor, Michigan.

The _____ interviews about 80,000 Americans annually and asks about their satisfaction with the goods and services they have consumed.

a. ADTECH
b. ACNielsen
c. AMAX
d. American Customer Satisfaction Index

6. Mystery shopping or Mystery Consumer is a tool used by market research companies to measure quality of retail service or gather specific information about products and services. _____ posing as normal customers perform specific tasks-- such as purchasing a product, asking questions, registering complaints or behaving in a certain way - and then provide detailed reports or feedback about their experiences.

Mystery shopping began in the 1940s as a way to measure employee integrity.

a. Questionnaire
b. Market research
c. Mystery shopping
d. Mystery shoppers

7. _____ is an advertisement in which a particular product specifically mentions a competitor by name for the express purpose of showing why the competitor is inferior to the product naming it.

This should not be confused with parody advertisements, where a fictional product is being advertised for the purpose of poking fun at the particular advertisement, nor should it be confused with the use of a coined brand name for the purpose of comparing the product without actually naming an actual competitor. ('Wikipedia tastes better and is less filling than the Encyclopedia Galactica.')

In the 1980s, during what has been referred to as the cola wars, soft-drink manufacturer Pepsi ran a series of advertisements where people, caught on hidden camera, in a blind taste test, chose Pepsi over rival Coca-Cola.

a. Comparative advertising
b. Cost per conversion
c. Heavy-up
d. GL-70

8. In marketing, customer _____, lifetime customer value (LCV), or _____ (LTV) and a new concept of 'customer life cycle management' is the present value of the future cash flows attributed to the customer relationship. Use of customer _____ as a marketing metric tends to place greater emphasis on customer service and long-term customer satisfaction, rather than on maximizing short-term sales.

Customer _____ has intuitive appeal as a marketing concept, because in theory it represents exactly how much each customer is worth in monetary terms, and therefore exactly how much a marketing department should be willing to spend to acquire each customer.

a. Brand infiltration
b. Lifetime value
c. Sweepstakes
d. Value chain

9. _____ is the difference between the revenues earned from and the costs associated with the customer relationship in a specified period.

According to Philip Kotler,'a profitable customer is a person, household or a company that overtime, yields a revenue stream that exceeds by an acceptable amount the company's cost stream of attracting, selling and servicing the customer'

Although _____ is nothing more than the result of applying the business concept of profit to a customer relationship, measuring the profitability of a firm's customers or customer groups can often deliver useful business insights.

Quite often a very small percentage of the firm's best customers will account for a large portion of firm profit.

- a. Power III
- b. 180SearchAssistant
- c. Cost management
- d. Customer profitability

10. Competitiveness is a comparative concept of the ability and performance of a firm, sub-sector or country to sell and supply goods and/or services in a given market. Although widely used in economics and business management, the usefulness of the concept, particularly in the context of national competitiveness, is vigorously disputed by economists, such as Paul Krugman .

The term may also be applied to markets, where it is used to refer to the extent to which the market structure may be regarded as perfectly _____.

- a. Customs union
- b. Geographical pricing
- c. Free trade zone
- d. Competitive

11. _____ is, in very basic words, a position a firm occupies against its competitors.

According to Michael Porter, the three methods for creating a sustainable _____ are through:

1. Cost leadership - Cost advantage occurs when a firm delivers the same services as its competitors but at a lower cost;

2.

- a. 180SearchAssistant
- b. Competitive advantage
- c. Power III
- d. 6-3-5 Brainwriting

12. A _____ is a collection of symbols, experiences and associations connected with a product, a service, a person or any other artifact or entity.

_____s have become increasingly important components of culture and the economy, now being described as 'cultural accessories and personal philosophies'.

Some people distinguish the psychological aspect of a _____ from the experiential aspect.

Chapter 5. Creating Customer Value, Satisfaction, and Loyalty

a. Brand equity
b. Brandable software
c. Store brand
d. Brand

13. _____ refers to the marketing effects or outcomes that accrue to a product with its brand name compared with those that would accrue if the same product did not have the brand name . And, at the root of these marketing effects is consumers' knowledge. In other words, consumers' knowledge about a brand makes manufacturers/advertisers respond differently or adopt appropriately adapt measures for the marketing of the brand .

a. Brand equity
b. Brand image
c. Brand aversion
d. Product extension

14.

The net present value (NPV) of all of a company's customers in terms of customer loyalty and indirectly, the revenue that the company can obtain from them.

In deciding the value of a company, it is important to know of how much value its customer base is in terms of future revenues. The greater the _____ , the more future revenue in the lifetime of its clients; this means that a company with a higher _____ can get more money from its customers on average than another company that is identical in all other characteristics.

a. Customer equity
b. Total cost
c. Product proliferation
d. Marginal revenue

15. _____ consists of the processes a company uses to track and organize its contacts with its current and prospective customers. _____ software is used to support these processes; information about customers and customer interactions can be entered, stored and accessed by employees in different company departments. Typical _____ goals are to improve services provided to customers, and to use customer contact information for targeted marketing.

a. Product bundling
b. Customer relationship management
c. Commercialization
d. Demand generation

16. _____ is a market coverage strategy in which a firm decides to ignore market segment differences and go after the whole market with one offer.it is type of marketing (or attempting to sell through persuasion) of a product to a wide audience. The idea is to broadcast a message that will reach the largest number of people possible. Traditionally _____ has focused on radio, television and newspapers as the medium used to reach this broad audience.

a. Cyberdoc
b. Marketspace
c. Mass marketing
d. Business-to-consumer

17. _____, in marketing, manufacturing, and management, is the use of flexible computer-aided manufacturing systems to produce custom output. Those systems combine the low unit costs of mass production processes with the flexibility of individual customization.

'_____' is the new frontier in business competition for both manufacturing and service industries.

Chapter 5. Creating Customer Value, Satisfaction, and Loyalty

   a. Power III
   c. Vertical integration
   b. Mass customization
   d. Flanking marketing warfare strategies

18. On an intranet or B2E Enterprise Web portals, personalization is often based on user attributes such as department, functional area, or role. The term _____ in this context refers to the ability of users to modify the page layout or specify what content should be displayed.

There are two categories of personalizations:

1. Rule-based
2. Content-based

Web personalization models include rules-based filtering, based on 'if this, then that' rules processing, and collaborative filtering, which serves relevant material to customers by combining their own personal preferences with the preferences of like-minded others. Collaborative filtering works well for books, music, video, etc.

   a. Self branding
   c. Cashmere Agency
   b. Movin'
   d. Customization

19. Customer _____ consists of the processes a company uses to track and organize its contacts with its current and prospective customers. CRelationship management software is used to support these processes; information about customers and customer interactions can be entered, stored and accessed by employees in different company departments. Typical CRelationship management goals are to improve services provided to customers, and to use customer contact information for targeted marketing.
   a. Product bundling
   c. Marketing
   b. Green marketing
   d. Relationship management

20. _____ refers to marketing strategies applied directly to a specific consumer.

Having the knowledge on the consumer preferences, there are suggested personalized products and promotions to each consumer.

The _____ is based in four main steps in order to fulfill its goals: Those stages are identify, differentiate, interact, and customize.

   a. ACNielsen
   c. AMAX
   b. One-to-one marketing
   d. ADTECH

21. _____ is defined by the American _____ Association as the activity, set of institutions, and processes for creating, communicating, delivering, and exchanging offerings that have value for customers, clients, partners, and society at large. The term developed from the original meaning which referred literally to going to market, as in shopping, or going to a market to sell goods or services.

_____ practice tends to be seen as a creative industry, which includes advertising, distribution and selling.

Chapter 5. Creating Customer Value, Satisfaction, and Loyalty

a. Customer acquisition management
c. Marketing

b. Marketing myopia
d. Product naming

22. A _____ is a plan of action designed to achieve a particular goal.

_____ is different from tactics. In military terms, tactics is concerned with the conduct of an engagement while _____ is concerned with how different engagements are linked.

a. Power III
c. Strategy

b. 180SearchAssistant
d. 6-3-5 Brainwriting

23. The _____ is the group of customers and/or consumers that a business serves. In the most situations, a large part of this group is made up of repeat customers with a high ratio of purchase over time. These customers are the main source of consumer spending.

a. Psychological pricing
c. First-mover advantage

b. Supplier diversity
d. Customer base

24. _____ is a form of marketing developed from direct response marketing campaigns conducted in the 1970's and 1980's which emphasizes customer retention and satisfaction, rather than a dominant focus on 'point of sale' transactions.

_____ differs from other forms of marketing in that it recognizes the long term value to the firm of keeping customers, as opposed to direct or 'Intrusion' marketing, which focuses upon acquisition of new clients by targeting majority demographics based upon prospective client lists.

_____ refers to long-term and mutually beneficial arrangement wherein both buyer and seller focus on value enhancement through the certain of more satisfying exchange. This approach attempts to transcend the simple purchase exchange process with customer to make more meaningful and richer contact by providing a more holistic, personalized purchase, and use orn consumption experience to create stronger ties.

a. Global marketing
c. Diversity marketing

b. Guerrilla Marketing
d. Relationship marketing

25. Electronic commerce, commonly known as _____ or eCommerce, consists of the buying and selling of products or services over electronic systems such as the Internet and other computer networks. The amount of trade conducted electronically has grown extraordinarily with wide-spread Internet usage. A wide variety of commerce is conducted in this way, spurring and drawing on innovations in electronic funds transfer, supply chain management, Internet marketing, online transaction processing, electronic data interchange (EDI), inventory management systems, and automated data collection systems.

a. ACNielsen
c. AMAX

b. ADTECH
d. E-commerce

26. A _____ is a structured collection of records or data that is stored in a computer system. The structure is achieved by organizing the data according to a _____ model. The model in most common use today is the relational model.

a. 6-3-5 Brainwriting
c. Power III

b. 180SearchAssistant
d. Database

Chapter 5. Creating Customer Value, Satisfaction, and Loyalty

27. _____ is a form of direct marketing using databases of customers or potential customers to generate personalized communications in order to promote a product or service for marketing purposes. The method of communication can be any addressable medium, as in direct marketing.

The distinction between direct and _____ stems primarily from the attention paid to the analysis of data.

a. Power III
c. Direct marketing
b. Direct Marketing Associations
d. Database marketing

28. _____ refer to a collection of facts usually collected as the result of experience, observation or experiment or a set of premises. This may consist of numbers, words particularly as measurements or observations of a set of variables. _____ are often viewed as a lowest level of abstraction from which information and knowledge are derived.

a. Pearson product-moment correlation coefficient
c. Mean
b. Sample size
d. Data

29. A _____ is a commercial building for storage of goods. _____s are used by manufacturers, importers, exporters, wholesalers, transport businesses, customs, etc. They are usually large plain buildings in industrial areas of cities and towns.

a. 6-3-5 Brainwriting
c. Warehouse
b. 180SearchAssistant
d. Power III

Chapter 6. Analyzing Consumer Markets

1. _____ is a broad label that refers to any individuals or households that use goods and services generated within the economy. The concept of a _____ is used in different contexts, so that the usage and significance of the term may vary.

A _____ is a person who uses any product or service.

a. Consumer
b. Power III
c. 6-3-5 Brainwriting
d. 180SearchAssistant

2. _____ is difficult to define. For example, in 1952, Alfred Kroeber and Clyde Kluckhohn compiled a list of 164 definitions of '_____' in _____: A Critical Review of Concepts and Definitions. However, the word '_____' is most commonly used in three basic senses:

- excellence of taste in the fine arts and humanities
- an integrated pattern of human knowledge, belief, and behavior that depends upon the capacity for symbolic thought and social learning
- the set of shared attitudes, values, goals, and practices that characterizes an institution, organization or group.

When the concept first emerged in eighteenth- and nineteenth-century Europe, it connoted a process of cultivation or improvement, as in agriculture or horticulture. In the nineteenth century, it came to refer first to the betterment or refinement of the individual, especially through education, and then to the fulfillment of national aspirations or ideals.

a. AStore
b. Albert Einstein
c. African Americans
d. Culture

3. In sociology, anthropology and cultural studies, a _____ is a group of people with a culture (whether distinct or hidden) which differentiates them from the larger culture to which they belong. If a particular _____ is characterized by a systematic opposition to the dominant culture, it may be described as a counterculture. As Ken Gelder notes, _____s are social, with their own shared conventions, values and rituals, but they can also seem 'immersed' or self-absorbed--another feature that distinguishes them from countercultures.

a. 180SearchAssistant
b. Subculture
c. Power III
d. 6-3-5 Brainwriting

4. _____ is the study of when, why, how, where and what people do or do not buy products. It blends elements from psychology, sociology, social psychology, anthropology and economics. It attempts to understand the buyer decision making process, both individually and in groups. It studies characteristics of individual consumers such as demographics and behavioural variables in an attempt to understand people's wants. It also tries to assess influences on the consumer from groups such as family, friends, reference groups, and society in general.

a. Consumer confidence
b. Multidimensional scaling
c. Communal marketing
d. Consumer behavior

5. _____ is defined by the American _____ Association as the activity, set of institutions, and processes for creating, communicating, delivering, and exchanging offerings that have value for customers, clients, partners, and society at large. The term developed from the original meaning which referred literally to going to market, as in shopping, or going to a market to sell goods or services.

_____ practice tends to be seen as a creative industry, which includes advertising, distribution and selling.

   a. Customer acquisition management
   c. Marketing myopia
   b. Product naming
   d. Marketing

6. _____ is a concept that arose out of the theory of two-step flow of communication propounded by Paul Lazarsfeld and Elihu Katz. This theory is one of several models that try to explain the diffusion of innovations, ideas, or commercial products.

The opinion leader is the agent who is an active media user and who interprets the meaning of media messages or content for lower-end media users.

   a. Elasticity
   c. Intellectual property
   b. ACNielsen
   d. Opinion leadership

7. A _____ is a sociological concept referring to a group to which an individual or another group is compared.

_____s are used in order to evaluate and determine the nature of a given individual or other group's characteristics and sociological attributes. It is the group to which the individual relates or aspires relate himself or self psychologically.

   a. Reference group
   c. Mociology
   b. Minority
   d. Power III

8. A _____ is a subgroup of people or organizations sharing one or more characteristics that cause them to have similar product and/or service needs. A true _____ meets all of the following criteria: it is distinct from other segments (different segments have different needs), it is homogeneous within the segment (exhibits common needs); it responds similarly to a market stimulus, and it can be reached by a market intervention. The term is also used when consumers with identical product and/or service needs are divided up into groups so they can be charged different amounts.
   a. Production orientation
   c. Commercial planning
   b. Customer insight
   d. Market segment

9. _____s is the social science that studies the production, distribution, and consumption of goods and services. The term _____s comes from the Ancient Greek οἰκονομία from οἶκος (oikos, 'house') + νόμος (nomos, 'custom' or 'law'), hence 'rules of the house(hold)'. Current _____ models developed out of the broader field of political economy in the late 19th century, owing to a desire to use an empirical approach more akin to the physical sciences.
   a. ACNielsen
   c. Economic
   b. Industrial organization
   d. ADTECH

10. A _____ is a collection of symbols, experiences and associations connected with a product, a service, a person or any other artifact or entity.

_____s have become increasingly important components of culture and the economy, now being described as 'cultural accessories and personal philosophies'.

Some people distinguish the psychological aspect of a _____ from the experiential aspect.

a. Brand
b. Brand equity
c. Brandable software
d. Store brand

11. _____ or self identity refers to the global understanding a sentient being has of him or herself. It presupposes but can be distinguished from self-consciousness, which is simply an awareness of one's self. It is also more general than self-esteem, which is the purely evaluative element of the _____.

a. 180SearchAssistant
b. Power III
c. Need for cognition
d. Self-concept

12. _____ was originally coined by Austrian psychologist Alfred Adler in 1929. The current broader sense of the word dates from 1961.

In sociology, a _____ is the way a person lives.

a. 180SearchAssistant
b. 6-3-5 Brainwriting
c. Power III
d. Lifestyle

13. _____ is a demographic defining a particular market segment related to sustainable living, 'green' ecological initiatives, and generally composed of a relatively upscale and well-educated population segment. Researchers have reported a range of sizes of the _____ market segment. For example, Worldwatch Institute reported that the _____ market segment in the year 2006 was estimated at $300 billion, approximately 30% of the USA consumer market; and, a study by the Natural Marketing Institute showed that in 2007, 40 million Americans were included within the _____ demographic.

a. Consumocracy
b. Product line extension
c. Gold Key Matching Service
d. Lifestyles of Health and Sustainability

14. A personal and cultural _____ is a relative ethic _____, an assumption upon which implementation can be extrapolated. A _____ system is a set of consistent _____s and measures that is soo not true. A principle _____ is a foundation upon which other _____s and measures of integrity are based.

a. Supreme Court of the United States
b. Package-on-Package
c. Perceptual maps
d. Value

15. A _____ is a plan of action designed to achieve a particular goal.

_____ is different from tactics. In military terms, tactics is concerned with the conduct of an engagement while _____ is concerned with how different engagements are linked.

a. Power III
b. 6-3-5 Brainwriting
c. 180SearchAssistant
d. Strategy

16. _____ is an investment technique that requires investors to purchase multiple financial products with different maturity dates.

Chapter 6. Analyzing Consumer Markets

_____ avoids the risk of reinvesting a big portion of assets in an unfavorable financial environment. For example, a person has both a 2015 matured CD and a 2018 matured CD.

a. 6-3-5 Brainwriting
c. Power III

b. 180SearchAssistant
d. Laddering

17. _____ is the set of reasons that determines one to engage in a particular behavior. The term is generally used for human _____ but, theoretically, it can be used to describe the causes for animal behavior as well

a. 180SearchAssistant
c. Power III

b. Role playing
d. Motivation

18. In psychology, philosophy, and the cognitive sciences, _____ is the process of attaining awareness or understanding of sensory information. It is a task far more complex than was imagined in the 1950s and 1960s, when it was predicted that building perceiving machines would take about a decade, a goal which is still very far from fruition. The word _____ comes from the Latin words _____, percepio, meaning 'receiving, collecting, action of taking possession, apprehension with the mind or senses.'

_____ is one of the oldest fields in psychology.

a. 180SearchAssistant
c. Groupthink

b. Power III
d. Perception

19. _____ is a term that refers to the tendency of people to interpret information in a way that will support what they already believe. This concept, along with selective attention and selective retention, makes it hard for marketers to get their message across and create good product perception.

a. Psychological Abstracts
c. Selective distortion

b. Power III
d. 180SearchAssistant

20. _____ is the process when people remember messages that are closer to their interests, values and beliefs more accurately, than those that are in contrast with their values and beliefs, selecting what to keep in the memory, narrowing the informational flow.

Such examples could include:

- A person may gradually reflect more positively on their time at school as they grow older
- A consumer might remember only the positive health benefits of a product they enjoy
- People tending to omit problems and disputes in past relationships
- A conspiracy theorist paying less attention to facts which do not aid their standpoint

a. Power III
c. 6-3-5 Brainwriting

b. Selective retention
d. 180SearchAssistant

21. _____ is the process of transforming information from one format into another. The opposite operation is called decoding.

There are a number of more specific meanings that apply in certain contexts:

- _____ is a basic perceptual process of interpreting incoming stimuli; technically speaking, it is a complex, multi-stage process of converting relatively objective sensory input (e.g., light, sound) into subjectively meaningful experience.
- A content format is a specific _____ format for converting a specific type of data to information.
- Character _____ is a code that pairs a set of natural language characters (such as an alphabet or syllabary) with a set of something else, such as numbers or electrical pulses.
- Text _____ uses a markup language to tag the structure and other features of a text to facilitate processing by computers.
- Semantics _____ of formal language A in formal language B is a method of representing all terms (e.g. programs or descriptions) of language A using language B.
- Electronic _____ transforms a signal into a code optimized for transmission or storage, generally done with a codec.
- Neural _____ is the way in which information is represented in neurons.
- Memory _____ is the process of converting sensations into memories.
- Encryption transforms information for secrecy.

    a. Encoding   b. ACNielsen
    c. AMAX   d. ADTECH

22. _____ is systematic determination of merit, worth, and significance of something or someone using criteria against a set of standards. _____ often is used to characterize and appraise subjects of interest in a wide range of human enterprises, including the arts, criminal justice, foundations and non-profit organizations, government, health care, and other human services.

Depending on the topic of interest, there are professional groups which look to the quality and rigor of the _____ process.

    a. ACNielsen   b. Evaluation
    c. AMAX   d. ADTECH

23. _____ can be regarded as an outcome of mental processes (cognitive process) leading to the selection of a course of action among several alternatives. Every _____ process produces a final choice. The output can be an action or an opinion of choice.
    a. Power III   b. 6-3-5 Brainwriting
    c. 180SearchAssistant   d. Decision making

24.

_____ is a systematic method to improve the 'value' of goods or products and services by using an examination of function. Value, as defined, is the ratio of function to cost. Value can therefore be increased by either improving the function or reducing the cost.

a. Power III
b. 180SearchAssistant
c. Productivity
d. Value engineering

25. _____ is the subjective judgment that people make about the characteristics and severity of a risk. The phrase is most commonly used in reference to natural hazards and threats to the environment or health, such as nuclear power. Several theories have been proposed to explain why different people make different estimates of the dangerousness of risks.
   a. 180SearchAssistant
   b. Power III
   c. 6-3-5 Brainwriting
   d. Risk perception

26. _____ is a concept that denotes the precise probability of specific eventualities. Technically, the notion of _____ is independent from the notion of value and, as such, eventualities may have both beneficial and adverse consequences. However, in general usage the convention is to focus only on potential negative impact to some characteristic of value that may arise from a future event.
   a. Risk
   b. 180SearchAssistant
   c. 6-3-5 Brainwriting
   d. Power III

27. A _____ is a process that can allow an organization to concentrate its limited resources on the greatest opportunities to increase sales and achieve a sustainable competitive advantage. A _____ should be centered around the key concept that customer satisfaction is the main goal.

A _____ is most effective when it is an integral component of corporate strategy, defining how the organization will successfully engage customers, prospects, and competitors in the market arena.

   a. Societal marketing
   b. Cyberdoc
   c. Psychographic
   d. Marketing strategy

28. _____ is a standard point of view or personal prejudice. especially when the tendency interferes with the ability to be impartial, unprejudiced, or objective. The term _____ed is used to describe an action, judgment, or other outcome influenced by a prejudged perspective.
   a. Bias
   b. 6-3-5 Brainwriting
   c. Power III
   d. 180SearchAssistant

29. _____ is a theory that describes decisions between alternatives that involve risk, i.e. alternatives with uncertain outcomes, where the probabilities are known. The model is descriptive: it tries to model real-life choices, rather than optimal decisions.

_____ was developed by Daniel Kahneman, professor at Princeton University's Department of Psychology, and Amos Tversky in 1979 as a psychologically realistic alternative to expected utility theory.

   a. 6-3-5 Brainwriting
   b. 180SearchAssistant
   c. Power III
   d. Prospect theory

Chapter 7. Analyzing Business Markets

1. _____ is a broad label that refers to any individuals or households that use goods and services generated within the economy. The concept of a _____ is used in different contexts, so that the usage and significance of the term may vary.

A _____ is a person who uses any product or service.

 a. 180SearchAssistant
 b. Power III
 c. 6-3-5 Brainwriting
 d. Consumer

2. In economics, _____ is the desire to own something and the ability to pay for it. The term _____ signifies the ability or the willingness to buy a particular commodity at a given point of time.

 a. Market dominance
 b. Discretionary spending
 c. Market system
 d. Demand

3. _____ is a term in economics, where demand for one good or service occurs as a result of demand for another. This may occur as the former is a part of production of the second. For example, demand for coal leads to _____ for mining, as coal must be mined for coal to be consumed.

 a. Power III
 b. 6-3-5 Brainwriting
 c. 180SearchAssistant
 d. Derived demand

4. In economics, _____ describes demand that is not very sensitive to a change in price.
 a. ACNielsen
 b. ADTECH
 c. AMAX
 d. Inelastic

5. A _____ is a business that is independently owned and operated, with a small number of employees and relatively low volume of sales. The legal definition of 'small' often varies by country and industry, but is generally under 100 employees in the United States and under 50 employees in the European Union. In comparison, the definition of mid-sized business by the number of employees is generally under 500 in the U.S. and 250 for the European Union.
 a. Time to market
 b. Small business
 c. Customer centricity
 d. Product support

6. A _____ is any systematic process enabling many market players to bid and ask: helping bidders and sellers interact and make deals. It is not just the price mechanism but the entire system of regulation, qualification, credentials, reputations and clearing that surrounds that mechanism and makes it operate in a social context.

Because a _____ relies on the assumption that players are constantly involved and unequally enabled, a _____ is distinguished specifically from a voting system where candidates seek the support of voters on a less regular basis.

 a. Market penetration
 b. Public market
 c. Perfect market
 d. Market system

Chapter 7. Analyzing Business Markets

7. A _____, in marketing, procurement, and organizational studies, is a group of employees, family members, or members of any type of organization responsible for purchasing an item for the organization. In a business setting, major purchases typically require input from various parts of the organization, including finance, accounting, purchasing, information technology management, and senior management. Highly technical purchases, such as information systems or production equipment, also require the expertise of technical specialists.

   a. Commercialization
   b. Marketing myopia
   c. Packshot
   d. Buying center

8. _____ is a concept that denotes the precise probability of specific eventualities. Technically, the notion of _____ is independent from the notion of value and, as such, eventualities may have both beneficial and adverse consequences. However, in general usage the convention is to focus only on potential negative impact to some characteristic of value that may arise from a future event.

   a. Risk
   b. Power III
   c. 6-3-5 Brainwriting
   d. 180SearchAssistant

9. _____ refers to a business or organization attempting to acquire goods or services to accomplish the goals of the enterprise. Though there are several organizations that attempt to set standards in the _____ process, processes can vary greatly between organizations. Typically the word '_____' is not used interchangeably with the word 'procurement', since procurement typically includes Expediting, Supplier Quality, and Traffic and Logistics (T'L) in addition to _____.

   a. Purchasing
   b. Supply chain
   c. Supply network
   d. Drop shipping

10. _____ is the business-to-business or business-to-consumer or Business-to-government purchase and sale of supplies, Work and services through the Internet as well as other information and networking systems, such as Electronic Data Interchange and Enterprise Resource Planning. Typically, _____ Web sites allow qualified and registered users to look for buyers or sellers of goods and services. Depending on the approach, buyers or sellers may specify costs or invite bids.

    a. ACNielsen
    b. E-procurement
    c. AMAX
    d. ADTECH

11. A _____ or logistics network is the system of organizations, people, technology, activities, information and resources involved in moving a product or service from supplier to customer. _____ activities transform natural resources, raw materials and components into a finished product that is delivered to the end customer. In sophisticated _____ systems, used products may re-enter the _____ at any point where residual value is recyclable.

    a. Supply chain network
    b. Supply chain
    c. Purchasing
    d. Demand chain management

12. _____ is a form of communication that typically attempts to persuade potential customers to purchase or to consume more of a particular brand of product or service. 'While now central to the contemporary global economy and the reproduction of global production networks, it is only quite recently that _____ has been more than a marginal influence on patterns of sales and production. The formation of modern _____ was intimately bound up with the emergence of new forms of monopoly capitalism around the end of the 19th and beginning of the 20th century as one element in corporate strategies to create, organize and where possible control markets, especially for mass produced consumer goods.

    a. ACNielsen
    b. Advertising
    c. ADTECH
    d. AMAX

Chapter 7. Analyzing Business Markets

13. A _____ is an explicit set of requirements to be satisfied by a material, product, or service.

In engineering, manufacturing, and business, it is vital for suppliers, purchasers, and users of materials, products, or services to understand and agree upon all requirements. A _____ is a type of a standard which is often referenced by a contract or procurement document.

   a. Specification
   b. New product development
   c. Product optimization
   d. Product development

14. A supply chain is the system of organizations, people, technology, activities, information and resources involved in moving a product or service from _____ to customer. Supply chain activities transform natural resources, raw materials and components into a finished product that is delivered to the end customer. In sophisticated supply chain systems, used products may re-enter the supply chain at any point where residual value is recyclable.
   a. Bringin' Home the Oil
   b. Product line extension
   c. Rebate
   d. Supplier

15. A personal and cultural _____ is a relative ethic _____, an assumption upon which implementation can be extrapolated. A _____ system is a set of consistent _____s and measures that is soo not true. A principle _____ is a foundation upon which other _____s and measures of integrity are based.
   a. Package-on-Package
   b. Supreme Court of the United States
   c. Perceptual maps
   d. Value

16.

_____ is a systematic method to improve the 'value' of goods or products and services by using an examination of function. Value, as defined, is the ratio of function to cost. Value can therefore be increased by either improving the function or reducing the cost.

   a. Power III
   b. Productivity
   c. Value engineering
   d. 180SearchAssistant

17. _____ is a term commonly used to describe commerce transactions between businesses like the one between a manufacturer and a wholesaler or a wholesaler and a retailer i.e both the buyer and the seller are business entity.This is unlike business-to-consumers (B2C) which involve a business entity and end consumer, or business-to-government (B2G) which involve a business entity and government.

The volume of B2B transactions is much higher than the volume of B2C transactions. The primary reason for this is that in a typical supply chain there will be many B2B transactions involving subcomponent or raw materials, and only one B2C transaction, specifically sale of the finished product to the end customer.

   a. Customer relationship management
   b. Disruptive technology
   c. Social marketing
   d. Business-to-business

Chapter 8. Identifying Market Segments and Targets

1. A _____ is a subgroup of people or organizations sharing one or more characteristics that cause them to have similar product and/or service needs. A true _____ meets all of the following criteria: it is distinct from other segments (different segments have different needs), it is homogeneous within the segment (exhibits common needs); it responds similarly to a market stimulus, and it can be reached by a market intervention. The term is also used when consumers with identical product and/or service needs are divided up into groups so they can be charged different amounts.
   - a. Commercial planning
   - b. Production orientation
   - c. Customer insight
   - d. Market segment

2. _____ is defined by the American _____ Association as the activity, set of institutions, and processes for creating, communicating, delivering, and exchanging offerings that have value for customers, clients, partners, and society at large. The term developed from the original meaning which referred literally to going to market, as in shopping, or going to a market to sell goods or services.

   _____ practice tends to be seen as a creative industry, which includes advertising, distribution and selling.
   - a. Customer acquisition management
   - b. Marketing myopia
   - c. Product naming
   - d. Marketing

3. _____ is a market coverage strategy in which a firm decides to ignore market segment differences and go after the whole market with one offer.it is type of marketing (or attempting to sell through persuasion) of a product to a wide audience. The idea is to broadcast a message that will reach the largest number of people possible. Traditionally _____ has focused on radio, television and newspapers as the medium used to reach this broad audience.
   - a. Business-to-consumer
   - b. Cyberdoc
   - c. Mass marketing
   - d. Marketspace

4. _____ is the practice of tailoring products, brands (microbrands), and promotions to meet the needs and wants of microsegments within a market. It is a type of market customization that deals with pricing of customer/product combinations at the store or individual level.

   Standard pricing policy ignores the differences in customer segments of specific stores within a regional chain of stores.
   - a. Soft sell
   - b. Micromarketing
   - c. Discontinuation
   - d. Chief privacy officer

5. In environmental modeling and especially in hydrology, a _____ model means a model that is acceptably consistent with observed natural processes, i.e. that simulates well, for example, observed river discharge. It is a key concept of the so-called Generalized Likelihood Uncertainty Estimation (GLUE) methodology to quantify how uncertain environmental predictions are.
   - a. 180SearchAssistant
   - b. Behavioral
   - c. 6-3-5 Brainwriting
   - d. Power III

6. _____ is an advertisement in which a particular product specifically mentions a competitor by name for the express purpose of showing why the competitor is inferior to the product naming it.

This should not be confused with parody advertisements, where a fictional product is being advertised for the purpose of poking fun at the particular advertisement, nor should it be confused with the use of a coined brand name for the purpose of comparing the product without actually naming an actual competitor. ('Wikipedia tastes better and is less filling than the Encyclopedia Galactica.')

In the 1980s, during what has been referred to as the cola wars, soft-drink manufacturer Pepsi ran a series of advertisements where people, caught on hidden camera, in a blind taste test, chose Pepsi over rival Coca-Cola.

a. Cost per conversion
b. Heavy-up
c. GL-70
d. Comparative advertising

7. _____ is the term used to describe the academic study of the various means by which individuals and entities relay information through mass media to large segments of the population at the same time. It is usually understood to relate to newspaper and magazine publishing, radio, television and film, as these are used both for disseminating news and for advertising.

_____ research includes media institutions and processes such as diffusion of information, and media effects such as persuasion or manipulation of public opinion.

a. Power III
b. Mass communication
c. 6-3-5 Brainwriting
d. 180SearchAssistant

8. _____ in its literal sense is the process of transformation of local or regional phenomena into global ones. It can be described as a process by which the people of the world are unified into a single society and function together.

This process is a combination of economic, technological, sociocultural and political forces.

a. Globalization
b. Power III
c. 180SearchAssistant
d. 6-3-5 Brainwriting

9. _____ is the sum of all experiences a customer has with a supplier of goods or services, over the duration of their relationship with that supplier. It can also be used to mean an individual experience over one transaction; the distinction is usually clear in context.

Analysts and commentators who write about _____ and CRM have increasingly recognized the importance of managing the customer's experience.

a. Customer service
b. Customer experience
c. Customer Integrated System
d. COPC Inc.

10. _____ is a neologism, defined as the combination of operational customization and marketing customization.

_____ is considered one of the key drivers underpinning the new economy. Most companies today are changing their marketing model from a seller-centric to a buyer-centric one.

a. Customerization
b. Product planning
c. Targeted advertising
d. Market intelligence

11. On an intranet or B2E Enterprise Web portals, personalization is often based on user attributes such as department, functional area, or role. The term _____ in this context refers to the ability of users to modify the page layout or specify what content should be displayed.

There are two categories of personalizations:

1. Rule-based
2. Content-based

Web personalization models include rules-based filtering, based on 'if this, then that' rules processing, and collaborative filtering, which serves relevant material to customers by combining their own personal preferences with the preferences of like-minded others. Collaborative filtering works well for books, music, video, etc.

a. Self branding
b. Customization
c. Movin'
d. Cashmere Agency

12. _____ is the study of the Earth and its lands, features, inhabitants, and phenomena. A literal translation would be 'to describe or write about the Earth'. The first person to use the word '_____' was Eratosthenes .
a. 180SearchAssistant
b. Power III
c. 6-3-5 Brainwriting
d. Geography

13. _____ or _____ data refers to selected population characteristics as used in government, marketing or opinion research, or the _____ profiles used in such research. Note the distinction from the term 'demography' Commonly-used _____ include race, age, income, disabilities, mobility (in terms of travel time to work or number of vehicles available), educational attainment, home ownership, employment status, and even location.
a. AStore
b. African Americans
c. Albert Einstein
d. Demographic

14. _____ is a term used to describe a person who was born during the demographic Post-World War II baby boom. Many analysts now believe that two distinct cultural generations were born during this baby boom; the older generation is often called the Baby Boom Generation and the younger generation is often called Generation Jones. The term '_____' is sometimes used in a cultural context, and sometimes used to describe someone who was born during the post-WWII baby boom.
a. Generation X
b. AStore
c. Greatest Generation
d. Baby boomer

15. _____ is a term used to identify people born after the post-World War II increase in birth rates (the baby boom) The term has been used in demography, the social sciences, and marketing, though it is most often used in popular culture.

In the U.S. _____ was originally referred to as the 'baby bust' generation because of the drop in the birth rate following the baby boom.

In the UK the term was first used in a 1964 study of British youth by Jane Deverson.

a. Generation X
b. Greatest Generation
c. AStore
d. Generation Y

16. _____ is a cohort which consists of those people born after the Generation X cohort. Its name is controversial and is synonymous with several alternative names including The Net Generation, Millennials, Echo Boomers, and iGeneration. _____ consists primarily of the offspring of the Generation Jones and Baby Boomers cohorts.
   a. Greatest Generation
   b. AStore
   c. Generation X
   d. Generation Y

17. The name _____ was coined in the November 5, 1951 cover story of Time to refer to the generation coming of age at the time, born during the Great Depression or World War II. The article, , found its characteristics as grave and fatalistic, conventional, possessing confused morals, expecting disappointment but desiring faith, and for women, desiring both a career and a family
   a. Power III
   b. 180SearchAssistant
   c. 6-3-5 Brainwriting
   d. Silent generation

18. In the field of marketing, demographics, opinion research, and social research in general, _____ variables are any attributes relating to personality, values, attitudes, interests, or lifestyles. They are also called IAO variables . They can be contrasted with demographic variables (such as age and gender), behavioral variables (such as usage rate or loyalty), and bizographic variables (such as industry, seniority and functional area.)
   a. Psychographic
   b. Lifetime value
   c. Marketing myopia
   d. Business-to-business

19. The acronym _____, is a psychographic segmentation. It was developed in the 1970s to explain changing U.S. values and lifestyles. It has since been reworked to enhance its ability to predict consumer behavior.

According to the _____ Framework, groups of people are arranged in a rectangle and are based on two dimensions. The vertical dimension segments people based on the degree to which they are innovative and have resources such as income, education, self-confidence, intelligence, leadership skills, and energy.

   a. 6-3-5 Brainwriting
   b. VALS
   c. 180SearchAssistant
   d. Power III

20. _____s are used in open sentences. For instance, in the formula x + 1 = 5, x is a _____ which represents an 'unknown' number. _____s are often represented by letters of the Roman alphabet, or those of other alphabets, such as Greek, and use other special symbols.
   a. Variable
   b. Quantitative
   c. Book of business
   d. Personalization

21. A _____ is a business that is independently owned and operated, with a small number of employees and relatively low volume of sales. The legal definition of 'small' often varies by country and industry, but is generally under 100 employees in the United States and under 50 employees in the European Union. In comparison, the definition of mid-sized business by the number of employees is generally under 500 in the U.S. and 250 for the European Union.
   a. Time to market
   b. Small business
   c. Customer centricity
   d. Product support

Chapter 8. Identifying Market Segments and Targets

22. The term _____ was first coined by New York Times best selling author, Linda Richardson. _____ emphasizes customer needs and meeting those needs with solutions combining products and/or services. A consultative salesperson typically provides detailed instruction or advice on which solution best meets these needs.
    a. Sales management
    b. Consultative selling
    c. Lead generation
    d. Request for proposal

23. _____ is a business term meaning the market segment to which a particular good or service is marketed. It is mainly defined by age, gender, geography, socio-economic grouping, technographic, or any other combination of demographics. It is generally studied and mapped by an organization through lists and reports containing demographic information that may have an effect on the marketing of key products or services.
    a. Market specialization
    b. Distribution
    c. Category Development Index
    d. Brando

24. In economics, business, retail, and accounting, a _____ is the value of money that has been used up to produce something, and hence is not available for use anymore. In economics, a _____ is an alternative that is given up as a result of a decision. In business, the _____ may be one of acquisition, in which case the amount of money expended to acquire it is counted as _____.
    a. Cost
    b. Fixed costs
    c. Variable cost
    d. Transaction cost

25. In marketing, _____ has come to mean the process by which marketers try to create an image or identity in the minds of their target market for its product, brand, or organization. It is the 'relative competitive comparison' their product occupies in a given market as perceived by the target market.

    Re-_____ involves changing the identity of a product, relative to the identity of competing products, in the collective minds of the target market.

    a. Moratorium
    b. Containerization
    c. GE matrix
    d. Positioning

Chapter 9. Creating Brand Equity

1. A _____ is a collection of symbols, experiences and associations connected with a product, a service, a person or any other artifact or entity.

   _____s have become increasingly important components of culture and the economy, now being described as 'cultural accessories and personal philosophies'.

   Some people distinguish the psychological aspect of a _____ from the experiential aspect.

   - a. Brandable software
   - b. Store brand
   - c. Brand equity
   - d. Brand

2. _____ is the application of marketing techniques to a specific product, product line, or brand. It seeks to increase the product's perceived value to the customer and thereby increase brand franchise and brand equity. Marketers see a brand as an implied promise that the level of quality people have come to expect from a brand will continue with future purchases of the same product.
   - a. Brand management
   - b. Naming rights
   - c. Store brand
   - d. Trademark distinctiveness

3. A _____ is a plan of action designed to achieve a particular goal.

   _____ is different from tactics. In military terms, tactics is concerned with the conduct of an engagement while _____ is concerned with how different engagements are linked.

   - a. 6-3-5 Brainwriting
   - b. Strategy
   - c. Power III
   - d. 180SearchAssistant

4. _____ refers to the marketing effects or outcomes that accrue to a product with its brand name compared with those that would accrue if the same product did not have the brand name . And, at the root of these marketing effects is consumers' knowledge. In other words, consumers' knowledge about a brand makes manufacturers/advertisers respond differently or adopt appropriately adapt measures for the marketing of the brand .
   - a. Brand image
   - b. Product extension
   - c. Brand aversion
   - d. Brand equity

5. _____ is defined by the American _____ Association as the activity, set of institutions, and processes for creating, communicating, delivering, and exchanging offerings that have value for customers, clients, partners, and society at large. The term developed from the original meaning which referred literally to going to market, as in shopping, or going to a market to sell goods or services.

   _____ practice tends to be seen as a creative industry, which includes advertising, distribution and selling.

   - a. Marketing myopia
   - b. Customer acquisition management
   - c. Product naming
   - d. Marketing

6. The _____ is a database of consumer perception of brands created and managed by BrandAsset Consulting, a division of Young ' Rubicam Brands to provide information to enable firms to improve the marketing decision-making process and to manage brands better. _____ and _____ also describe the Y'R group managing the database.

Chapter 9. Creating Brand Equity

_____ measures the value of a brand along four dimensions: 'Differentiation,' 'Relevance,' 'Esteem,' and 'Knowledge.' Differentiation and Relevance build up to 'Brand Strength.' Esteem and Knowledge are used to calculate 'Brand Stature.' _____ defines these terms as follows.

- a. Target audience
- b. Brand asset valuator
- c. Hoover free flights promotion
- d. Targeted advertising

7. A _____ is typically the attributes one associates with a brand, how the brand owner wants the consumer to perceive the brand - and by extension the branded company, organization, product or service. The brand owner will seek to bridge the gap between the _____ and the brand identity.
- a. Status brand
- b. Brand equity
- c. Brand loyalty
- d. Brand image

8. _____ or personalisation is tailoring a consumer product, electronic or written medium to a user based on personal details or characteristics they provide. More recently, it has especially been applied in the context of the World Wide Web.

Web pages are personalized based on the interests of an individual.

- a. Complex sale
- b. Sexism,
- c. Personalization
- d. Flighting

9. _____ , according to The American Marketing Association, is 'a planning process designed to assure that all brand contacts received by a customer or prospect for a product, service, or organization are relevant to that person and consistent over time.' (Marketing Power Dictionary)

_____ is a term used to describe a holistic approach to marketing. It aims to ensure consistency of message and the complementary use of media. The concept includes online and offline marketing channels.

- a. ADTECH
- b. ACNielsen
- c. Integrated marketing communications
- d. AMAX

10. _____ is a term used in marketing in general and e-marketing specifically. Marketers will ask permission before advancing to the next step in the purchasing process. For example, they ask permission to send advertisements to prospective customers.
- a. Spam Lit
- b. Personalized marketing
- c. Permission marketing
- d. Live banner

11. _____ is a marketing concept that refers to a consumer knowing of a brand's existence; at aggregate (brand) level it refers to the proportion of consumers who know of the brand.

Chapter 9. Creating Brand Equity

_____ can be measured by showing a consumer the brand and asking whether or not they knew of it beforehand. However, in common market research practice a variety of recognition and recall measures of _____ are employed all of which test the brand name's association to a product category cue, this came about because most market research in the 20th Century was conducted by post or telephone, actually showing the brand to consumers usually required more expensive face-to-face interviews (until web-based interviews became possible.)

   a. Brand orientation   b. Brand awareness
   c. Fitting Group   d. Brand equity

12. A personal and cultural _____ is a relative ethic _____, an assumption upon which implementation can be extrapolated. A _____ system is a set of consistent _____s and measures that is soo not true. A principle _____ is a foundation upon which other _____s and measures of integrity are based.

   a. Perceptual maps   b. Package-on-Package
   c. Supreme Court of the United States   d. Value

13. The _____ is a concept from business management that was first described and popularized by Michael Porter in his 1985 best-seller, Competitive Advantage: Creating and Sustaining Superior Performance.

A _____ is a chain of activities. Products pass through all activities of the chain in order and at each activity the product gains some value.

   a. Relationship management   b. Business-to-business
   c. Mass marketing   d. Value chain

14. The general definition of an _____ is an evaluation of a person, organization, system, process, project or product. _____s are performed to ascertain the validity and reliability of information; also to provide an assessment of a system's internal control. The goal of an _____ is to express an opinion on the person/organization/system (etc) in question, under evaluation based on work done on a test basis.

   a. AMAX   b. Audit
   c. ADTECH   d. ACNielsen

15. _____ is a list for goods and materials held available in stock by a business. It is also used for a list of the contents of a household and for a list for testamentary purposes of the possessions of someone who has died. In accounting _____ is considered an asset.

   a. Ending Inventory   b. ACNielsen
   c. ADTECH   d. Inventory

16. In operant conditioning, _____ occurs when an event following a response causes an increase in the probability of that response occurring in the future. Response strength can be assessed by measures such as the frequency with which the response is made (for example, a pigeon may peck a key more times in the session), or the speed with which it is made (for example, a rat may run a maze faster.) The environment change contingent upon the response is called a reinforcer.

   a. Generic brands   b. Relationship Management Application
   c. Completely randomized designs   d. Reinforcement

Chapter 9. Creating Brand Equity

17. _____ or brand stretching is a marketing strategy in which a firm marketing a product with a well-developed image uses the same brand name in a different product category. Organizations use this strategy to increase and leverage brand equity (definition: the net worth and long-term sustainability just from the renowned name.) An example of a _____ is Jello-gelatin creating Jello pudding pops.
   a. Brand extension
   b. Web 2.0
   c. Brand awareness
   d. Brand orientation

18. A product _____ is the use of an established product's brand name for a new item in the same product category. _____ s occur when a company introduces additional items in the same product category under the same brand name such as new flavors, forms, colors, added ingredients, package sizes.Examples includei) Zen LXI, Zen VXIii) Surf, Surf Excel, Surf Excel Blueiii) Splendour, Splendour Plusiv) Coke, Diet Coke, Vanilla Cokev) Clinic All Clear, Clinic Plus

   - brand
   - brand management
   - marketing
   - product management
   - Product lining

   a. Brand Development Index
   b. Targeted advertising
   c. Line extension
   d. Perishability

19. A _____ is the use of an established product's brand name for a new item in the same product category. _____ s occur when a company introduces additional items in the same product category under the same brand name such as new flavors, forms, colors, added ingredients, package sizes.
   a. Retail floor planning
   b. Product line extension
   c. Comparison-Shopping agent
   d. Pearson's chi-square

20. _____ is a trademark law concept permitting the owner of a famous trademark to forbid others from using that mark in a way that would lessen its uniqueness. In most cases, _____ involves an unauthorized use of another's trademark on products that do not compete with, and have little connection with, those of the trademark owner. For example, a famous trademark used by one company to refer to hair care products might be diluted if another company began using a similar mark to refer to breakfast cereals or spark plugs.
   a. Federal Bureau of Investigation
   b. Trademark attorney
   c. Trespass to land
   d. Trademark dilution

21. In business, a _____ is a product or a business unit that generates unusually high profit margins: so high that it is responsible for a large amount of a company's operating profit. This profit far exceeds the amount necessary to maintain the _____ business, and the excess is used by the business for other purposes.

A firm is said to be acting as a _____ when its earnings per share (EPS) is equal to its dividends per share (DPS), or in other words, when a firm pays out 100% of its free cash flow (FCF) to its shareholders as dividends at the end of each accounting term.

a. Crisis management
c. Goal setting
b. Corporate transparency
d. Cash cow

Chapter 10. Crafting the Brand Positioning

1. A _____ is a collection of symbols, experiences and associations connected with a product, a service, a person or any other artifact or entity.

_____s have become increasingly important components of culture and the economy, now being described as 'cultural accessories and personal philosophies'.

Some people distinguish the psychological aspect of a _____ from the experiential aspect.

   a. Brandable software
   c. Brand equity
   b. Store brand
   d. Brand

2. In marketing, _____ has come to mean the process by which marketers try to create an image or identity in the minds of their target market for its product, brand, or organization. It is the 'relative competitive comparison' their product occupies in a given market as perceived by the target market.

Re-_____ involves changing the identity of a product, relative to the identity of competing products, in the collective minds of the target market.

   a. GE matrix
   c. Moratorium
   b. Containerization
   d. Positioning

3. A _____ is a plan of action designed to achieve a particular goal.

_____ is different from tactics. In military terms, tactics is concerned with the conduct of an engagement while _____ is concerned with how different engagements are linked.

   a. Power III
   c. Strategy
   b. 6-3-5 Brainwriting
   d. 180SearchAssistant

4. A personal and cultural _____ is a relative ethic _____, an assumption upon which implementation can be extrapolated. A _____ system is a set of consistent _____s and measures that is soo not true. A principle _____ is a foundation upon which other _____s and measures of integrity are based.
   a. Value
   c. Perceptual maps
   b. Supreme Court of the United States
   d. Package-on-Package

5. In the field of marketing, a customer _____ consists of the sum total of benefits which a vendor promises that a customer will receive in return for the customer's associated payment (or other value-transfer.)

Put simply, the _____ is what the customer gets for his money.

Accordingly, a customer can evaluate a company's value-proposition on two broad dimensions with multiple subsets:

1. relative performance: what the customer gets from the vendor relative to a competitor's offering;
2. price: which consists of the payment the customer makes to acquire the product or service; plus the access cost

The vendor-company's marketing and sales efforts offer a customer _____; the vendor-company's delivery and customer-service processes then fulfill that value-proposition.

A value-proposition can assist in a firm's marketing strategy, and may guide a business to target a particular market segment.

    a. DefCom Australia
    b. Marketing performance measurement and management
    c. Relationship management
    d. Value proposition

6. Competitiveness is a comparative concept of the ability and performance of a firm, sub-sector or country to sell and supply goods and/or services in a given market. Although widely used in economics and business management, the usefulness of the concept, particularly in the context of national competitiveness, is vigorously disputed by economists, such as Paul Krugman .

The term may also be applied to markets, where it is used to refer to the extent to which the market structure may be regarded as perfectly _____.

    a. Competitive
    b. Free trade zone
    c. Geographical pricing
    d. Customs union

7. Trademark _____ is an important concept in the law governing trademarks and service marks. A trademark may be eligible for registration, or registrable, if amongst other things it performs the essential trademark function, and has distinctive character. Registrability can be understood as a continuum, with 'inherently distinctive' marks at one end, 'generic' and 'descriptive' marks with no distinctive character at the other end, and 'suggestive' and 'arbitrary' marks lying between these two points.

    a. Brand ambassador
    b. Distinctiveness
    c. Corporate colours
    d. Brand implementation

8. In marketing, _____ is the process of distinguishing the differences of a product or offering from others, to make it more attractive to a particular target market. This involves differentiating it from competitors' products as well as one's own product offerings.

Differentiation is a source of competitive advantage.

Chapter 10. Crafting the Brand Positioning

a. Corporate image
b. Packshot
c. Marketing myopia
d. Product differentiation

9. _____ Management is the succession of strategies used by management as a product goes through its _____. The conditions in which a product is sold changes over time and must be managed as it moves through its succession of stages.

The _____ goes through many phases, involves many professional disciplines, and requires many skills, tools and processes.

a. Chain stores
b. Supplier diversity
c. Product life cycle
d. Customer satisfaction

10. _____ is defined by the American _____ Association as the activity, set of institutions, and processes for creating, communicating, delivering, and exchanging offerings that have value for customers, clients, partners, and society at large. The term developed from the original meaning which referred literally to going to market, as in shopping, or going to a market to sell goods or services.

_____ practice tends to be seen as a creative industry, which includes advertising, distribution and selling.

a. Marketing myopia
b. Customer acquisition management
c. Product naming
d. Marketing

11. A _____ is a process that can allow an organization to concentrate its limited resources on the greatest opportunities to increase sales and achieve a sustainable competitive advantage. A _____ should be centered around the key concept that customer satisfaction is the main goal.

A _____ is most effective when it is an integral component of corporate strategy, defining how the organization will successfully engage customers, prospects, and competitors in the market arena.

a. Cyberdoc
b. Psychographic
c. Societal marketing
d. Marketing strategy

12. A craze is a product, idea, cultural movement, or model that gains popularity among a small section of the populace then quickly migrates to the mainstream. Crazes are characterized by their lightning fast adoption and swift departure from public awareness. Crazes and _____s are also characterized by their unusually high interest and sales figures relative to the time they are active in the marketplace, as compared with other similar products, ideas, cultural movements or models.

a. Power III
b. Fad
c. 6-3-5 Brainwriting
d. 180SearchAssistant

13. An _____ is a person who creates or discovers a new method, form, device or other useful means. The word _____ comes form the latin verb invenire, invent-, to find. The system of patents was established to encourage _____s by granting limited-term, limited monopoly on inventions determined to be sufficiently novel, non-obvious, and useful.

a. AMAX
b. ADTECH
c. ACNielsen
d. Inventor

14. _____ is the process or cycle of introducing a new product into the market. The actual launch of a new product is the final stage of new product development, and the one where the most money will have to be spent for advertising, sales promotion, and other marketing efforts. In the case of a new consumer packaged good, costs will be at least $ 10 million, but can reach up to $ 200 million.
   a. Commercialization
   b. Confusion marketing
   c. Sweepstakes
   d. Customer Interaction Tracker

15. Quality management can be considered to have three main components: quality control, quality assurance and _____. Quality management is focused not only on product quality, but also the means to achieve it. Quality management therefore uses quality assurance and control of processes as well as products to achieve more consistent quality.
   a. 6-3-5 Brainwriting
   b. Power III
   c. 180SearchAssistant
   d. Quality improvement

16. _____ is a rivalry between individuals, groups, nations for territory, a niche, or allocation of resources. It arises whenever two or more parties strive for a goal which cannot be shared. _____ occurs naturally between living organisms which co-exist in the same environment.
   a. Price competition
   b. Price fixing
   c. Competition
   d. Non-price competition

Chapter 11. Dealing with Competition

1. _____ is a rivalry between individuals, groups, nations for territory, a niche, or allocation of resources. It arises whenever two or more parties strive for a goal which cannot be shared. _____ occurs naturally between living organisms which co-exist in the same environment.

   a. Non-price competition
   b. Competition
   c. Price fixing
   d. Price competition

2. Competitiveness is a comparative concept of the ability and performance of a firm, sub-sector or country to sell and supply goods and/or services in a given market. Although widely used in economics and business management, the usefulness of the concept, particularly in the context of national competitiveness, is vigorously disputed by economists, such as Paul Krugman .

   The term may also be applied to markets, where it is used to refer to the extent to which the market structure may be regarded as perfectly _____.

   a. Customs union
   b. Geographical pricing
   c. Competitive
   d. Free trade zone

3. _____ in its literal sense is the process of transformation of local or regional phenomena into global ones. It can be described as a process by which the people of the world are unified into a single society and function together.

   This process is a combination of economic, technological, sociocultural and political forces.

   a. 6-3-5 Brainwriting
   b. 180SearchAssistant
   c. Power III
   d. Globalization

4. An _____ is the manufacturing of a good or service within a category. Although _____ is a broad term for any kind of economic production, in economics and urban planning _____ is a synonym for the secondary sector, which is a type of economic activity involved in the manufacturing of raw materials into goods and products.

   There are four key industrial economic sectors: the primary sector, largely raw material extraction industries such as mining and farming; the secondary sector, involving refining, construction, and manufacturing; the tertiary sector, which deals with services (such as law and medicine) and distribution of manufactured goods; and the quaternary sector, a relatively new type of knowledge _____ focusing on technological research, design and development such as computer programming, and biochemistry.

   a. AMAX
   b. ACNielsen
   c. ADTECH
   d. Industry

5. _____ is a common market form. Many markets can be considered monopolistically competitive, often including the markets for restaurants, cereal, clothing, shoes and service industries in large cities. Short-run equilibrium of the firm under _____

Monopolistically competitive markets have the following characteristics:

- There are many producers and many consumers in a given market, and no business has total control over the market price.
- Consumers perceive that there are non-price differences among the competitors' products.
- There are few barriers to entry and exit.
- Producers have a degree of control over price.

Long-run equilibrium of the firm under _____

The characteristics of a monopolistically competitive market are almost the same as in perfect competition, with the exception of heterogeneous products, and that _____ involves a great deal of non-price competition (based on subtle product differentiation.) A firm making profits in the short run will break even in the long run because demand will decrease and average total cost will increase.

 a. Gross domestic product   b. Macroeconomics
 c. Monopolistic competition   d. Recession

6. An _____ is a market form in which a market or industry is dominated by a small number of sellers (oligopolists.) Because there are few participants in this type of market, each oligopolist is aware of the actions of the others. The decisions of one firm influence, and are influenced by, the decisions of other firms.
 a. ADTECH   b. AMAX
 c. ACNielsen   d. Oligopoly

7. In economics, a _____ exists when a specific individual or enterprise has sufficient control over a particular product or service to determine significantly the terms on which other individuals shall have access to it. Monopolies are thus characterized by a lack of economic competition for the good or service that they provide and a lack of viable substitute goods. The verb 'monopolize' refers to the process by which a firm gains persistently greater market share than what is expected under perfect competition.
 a. 6-3-5 Brainwriting   b. 180SearchAssistant
 c. Power III   d. Monopoly

8. In microeconomics and management, the term _____ describes a style of management control. Vertically integrated companies are united through a hierarchy with a common owner. Usually each member of the hierarchy produces a different product or (market-specific) service, and the products combine to satisfy a common need.
 a. Mass customization   b. Power III
 c. Flanking marketing warfare strategies   d. Vertical integration

9. A _____ is a concept used in strategic management that groups companies within an industry that have similar business models or similar combinations of strategies. For example, the restaurant industry can be divided into several _____s including fast-food and fine-dining based on variables such as preparation time, pricing, and presentation. The number of groups within an industry and their composition depends on the dimensions used to define the groups.
 a. Strategic business unit   b. Corporate strategy
 c. Strategic group   d. Switching cost

10. A _____ is a plan of action designed to achieve a particular goal.

_____ is different from tactics. In military terms, tactics is concerned with the conduct of an engagement while _____ is concerned with how different engagements are linked.

a. Power III
b. 6-3-5 Brainwriting
c. 180SearchAssistant
d. Strategy

11. _____, in strategic management and marketing, is the percentage or proportion of the total available market or market segment that is being serviced by a company. It can be expressed as a company's sales revenue (from that market) divided by the total sales revenue available in that market. It can also be expressed as a company's unit sales volume (in a market) divided by the total volume of units sold in that market.

a. Cyberdoc
b. Demand generation
c. Customer relationship management
d. Market share

12. _____ is a measure of the strength of a brand, product, service relative to competitive offerings. There is often a geographic element to the competitive landscape. In defining _____, you must see to what extent a product, brand, or firm controls a product category in a given geographic area.

a. Productivity
b. Market dominance
c. Discretionary spending
d. Market system

13. _____ is defined by the American _____ Association as the activity, set of institutions, and processes for creating, communicating, delivering, and exchanging offerings that have value for customers, clients, partners, and society at large. The term developed from the original meaning which referred literally to going to market, as in shopping, or going to a market to sell goods or services.

_____ practice tends to be seen as a creative industry, which includes advertising, distribution and selling.

a. Marketing myopia
b. Customer acquisition management
c. Product naming
d. Marketing

14. A _____ is a collection of symbols, experiences and associations connected with a product, a service, a person or any other artifact or entity.

_____s have become increasingly important components of culture and the economy, now being described as 'cultural accessories and personal philosophies'.

Some people distinguish the psychological aspect of a _____ from the experiential aspect.

a. Store brand
b. Brand
c. Brandable software
d. Brand equity

Chapter 12. Setting Product Strategy

1. In marketing, a _____ is a generic product augmented by everything that is needed for the customer to have a compelling reason to buy. The generic product is what is usually shipped to the customer. The _____ typically augments the generic product with training and support, manuals, cables, additional software or hardware, installation instructions, professional services, etc.
   a. Whole product
   b. Jobbing house
   c. Mass market
   d. Teaser rate

2. A personal and cultural _____ is a relative ethic _____, an assumption upon which implementation can be extrapolated. A _____ system is a set of consistent _____s and measures that is soo not true. A principle _____ is a foundation upon which other _____s and measures of integrity are based.
   a. Value
   b. Supreme Court of the United States
   c. Perceptual maps
   d. Package-on-Package

3. _____ is anything that is intended to save time, energy or frustration. A _____ store at a petrol station, for example, sells items that have nothing to do with gasoline/petrol, but it saves the consumer from having to go to a grocery store. '_____' is a very relative term and its meaning tends to change over time.
   a. Marketing buzz
   b. Demographic profile
   c. MaxDiff
   d. Convenience

4. In economics, a _____ or a hard good is a good which does not quickly wear out it yields services or utility over time rather than being completely used up when used once. Most goods are therefore _____s to a certain degree. These are goods that can last for a relatively long time, such as refrigerators, cars, and DVD players.
   a. Free good
   b. Power III
   c. Luxury good
   d. Durable good

5. An _____ is an unplanned or otherwise spontaneous purchase. One who tends to make such purchases is referred to as an impulse purchaser or impulse buyer.

Marketers and retailers tend to exploit these impulses which are tied to the basic want for instant gratification.

   a. ADTECH
   b. Impulse purchase
   c. ACNielsen
   d. AMAX

6. A _____ is something that is acted upon or used by or by human labour or industry, for use as a building material to create some product or structure. Often the term is used to denote material that came from nature and is in an unprocessed or minimally processed state. Iron ore, logs, and crude oil, would be examples.
   a. 180SearchAssistant
   b. Power III
   c. 6-3-5 Brainwriting
   d. Raw material

7. _____ is an advertisement in which a particular product specifically mentions a competitor by name for the express purpose of showing why the competitor is inferior to the product naming it.

This should not be confused with parody advertisements, where a fictional product is being advertised for the purpose of poking fun at the particular advertisement, nor should it be confused with the use of a coined brand name for the purpose of comparing the product without actually naming an actual competitor. ('Wikipedia tastes better and is less filling than the Encyclopedia Galactica.')

In the 1980s, during what has been referred to as the cola wars, soft-drink manufacturer Pepsi ran a series of advertisements where people, caught on hidden camera, in a blind taste test, chose Pepsi over rival Coca-Cola.

   a. Cost per conversion
   c. Heavy-up
   b. GL-70
   d. Comparative advertising

8. _____ is the examining of goods or services from retailers with the intent to purchase at that time. _____ is an activity of selection and/or purchase. In some contexts it is considered a leisure activity as well as an economic one.
   a. Hawkers
   c. Discount store
   b. Khodebshchik
   d. Shopping

9. In marketing, _____ is the process of distinguishing the differences of a product or offering from others, to make it more attractive to a particular target market. This involves differentiating it from competitors' products as well as one's own product offerings.

Differentiation is a source of competitive advantage.

   a. Corporate image
   c. Marketing myopia
   b. Packshot
   d. Product Differentiation

10. _____ is one of the four Ps of the marketing mix. The other three aspects are product, promotion, and place. It is also a key variable in microeconomic price allocation theory.
   a. Competitor indexing
   c. Price
   b. Relationship based pricing
   d. Pricing

11. _____ refers to several different marketing arrangements:

_____ is when two companies form an alliance to work together, creating marketing synergy. As described in _____: The Science of Alliance:

_____ is an arrangement that associates a single product or service with more than one brand name, or otherwise associates a product with someone other than the principal producer. The typical _____ agreement involves two or more companies acting in cooperation to associate any of various logos, color schemes, or brand identifiers to a specific product that is contractually designated for this purpose.

   a. Brand Development Index
   c. Target audience
   b. Line extension
   d. Co-branding

12. The _____ is a US law that applies to labels on many consumer products. It requires the label to state:

   - The identity of the product;
   - The name and place of business of the manufacturer, packer, or distributor; and
   - The net quantity of contents.

Chapter 12. Setting Product Strategy

The contents statement must include both metric and U.S. customary units.

Passed under Lyndon B. Johnson in 1966, the law first took effect on July 1, 1967. The metric labeling requirement was added in 1992 and took effect on February 14, 1994.

a. 6-3-5 Brainwriting
c. 180SearchAssistant
b. Fair Packaging and Labeling Act
d. Power III

13. The _____ is an independent agency of the United States government, established in 1914 by the _____ Act. Its principal mission is the promotion of 'consumer protection' and the elimination and prevention of what regulators perceive to be harmfully 'anti-competitive' business practices, such as coercive monopoly.

The _____ Act was one of President Wilson's major acts against trusts.

a. 6-3-5 Brainwriting
c. Power III
b. 180SearchAssistant
d. Federal Trade Commission

14. The _____ of 1914 (15 U.S.C §§ 41-58, as amended) established the Federal Trade Commission (FTC), a bipartisan body of five members appointed by the President of the United States for seven year terms. This Commission was authorized to issue Cease and Desist orders to large corporations to curb unfair trade practices. This Act also gave more flexibility to the US congress for judicial matters.

a. Product liability
c. Comparative negligence
b. Gripe site
d. Federal Trade Commission Act

15. An _____ is quite usually a standard guarantee from the seller of a product that specifies the extent to which the quality or performance of the product is assured and states the conditions under which the product can be returned, replaced, or repaired. It is often given in the form of a specific, written 'Warranty' document. However, a warranty may also arise by operation of law based upon the seller's description of the goods, and perhaps their source and quality, and any material deviation from that specification would violate the guarantee.

a. Imperial Group v. Philip Morris
c. Office for Harmonization in the Internal Market
b. Energy Star
d. Express warranty

Chapter 13. Designing and Managing Services

1. _____ is an advertisement in which a particular product specifically mentions a competitor by name for the express purpose of showing why the competitor is inferior to the product naming it.

This should not be confused with parody advertisements, where a fictional product is being advertised for the purpose of poking fun at the particular advertisement, nor should it be confused with the use of a coined brand name for the purpose of comparing the product without actually naming an actual competitor. ('Wikipedia tastes better and is less filling than the Encyclopedia Galactica.')

In the 1980s, during what has been referred to as the cola wars, soft-drink manufacturer Pepsi ran a series of advertisements where people, caught on hidden camera, in a blind taste test, chose Pepsi over rival Coca-Cola.

a. GL-70
b. Cost per conversion
c. Heavy-up
d. Comparative advertising

2. _____ is used in marketing to describe a key quality of services as distinct from goods. _____ is the characteristic that a service has which renders it impossible to divorce the supply or production of the service from its consumption.

Other key characteristics of services include perishability, intangibility and variability.

a. Inseparability
b. Individual branding
c. Online focus group
d. Engagement

3. _____ is used in marketing to describe the inability to assess the value gained from engaging in an activity using any tangible evidence. It is often used to describe services where there isn't a tangible product that the customer can purchase, that can be seen, tasted or touched.

Other key characteristics of services include perishability, inseparability and variability.

a. Individual branding
b. Automated surveys
c. Inseparability
d. Intangibility

4. _____ is used in marketing to describe the way in which service capacity cannot be stored for sale in the future. It is a key concept of services marketing.

Other key characteristics of services include intangibility, inseparability and variability.

a. Perishability
b. Specialty catalogs
c. National brand
d. Demonstrator model

5. _____ is the provision of service to customers before, during and after a purchase.

According to Turban et al., '_____ is a series of activities designed to enhance the level of customer satisfaction - that is, the feeling that a product or service has met the customer expectation.'

Its importance varies by product, industry and customer.

Chapter 13. Designing and Managing Services

a. COPC Inc.
b. Customer service
c. Customer experience
d. Facing

6. _____ is defined by the American _____ Association as the activity, set of institutions, and processes for creating, communicating, delivering, and exchanging offerings that have value for customers, clients, partners, and society at large. The term developed from the original meaning which referred literally to going to market, as in shopping, or going to a market to sell goods or services.

_____ practice tends to be seen as a creative industry, which includes advertising, distribution and selling.

a. Marketing
b. Product naming
c. Marketing myopia
d. Customer acquisition management

7. A _____ is a process that can allow an organization to concentrate its limited resources on the greatest opportunities to increase sales and achieve a sustainable competitive advantage. A _____ should be centered around the key concept that customer satisfaction is the main goal.

A _____ is most effective when it is an integral component of corporate strategy, defining how the organization will successfully engage customers, prospects, and competitors in the market arena.

a. Marketing strategy
b. Psychographic
c. Cyberdoc
d. Societal marketing

8. A personal and cultural _____ is a relative ethic _____, an assumption upon which implementation can be extrapolated. A _____ system is a set of consistent _____s and measures that is soo not true. A principle _____ is a foundation upon which other _____s and measures of integrity are based.

a. Value
b. Supreme Court of the United States
c. Perceptual maps
d. Package-on-Package

9. _____ is a broad label that refers to any individuals or households that use goods and services generated within the economy. The concept of a _____ is used in different contexts, so that the usage and significance of the term may vary.

A _____ is a person who uses any product or service.

a. Power III
b. 180SearchAssistant
c. 6-3-5 Brainwriting
d. Consumer

10. _____ is the study of when, why, how, where and what people do or do not buy products. It blends elements from psychology, sociology, social psychology, anthropology and economics. It attempts to understand the buyer decision making process, both individually and in groups. It studies characteristics of individual consumers such as demographics and behavioural variables in an attempt to understand people's wants. It also tries to assess influences on the consumer from groups such as family, friends, reference groups, and society in general.

a. Multidimensional scaling
b. Consumer confidence
c. Communal marketing
d. Consumer behavior

Chapter 13. Designing and Managing Services

11. _____ is a term used in business to describe the process of capturing a customer's requirements. Specifically, the _____ is a market research technique that produces a detailed set of customer wants and needs, organized into a hierarchical structure, and then prioritized in terms of relative importance and satisfaction with current alternatives. _____ studies typically consist of both qualitative and quantitative research steps.

   a. Corporate transparency
   b. Voice of the customer
   c. Crisis management
   d. Digital strategy

12. In the Mediterranean Basin and the Near East, a _____ is a small, separated garden pavilion open on some or all sides. _____s were common in Persia, India, Pakistan, and in the Ottoman Empire from the 13th century onward. Today, there are many _____s in and around the Topkapı Palace in Istanbul, and they are still a relatively common sight in Greece.

   a. 180SearchAssistant
   b. 6-3-5 Brainwriting
   c. Power III
   d. Kiosk

13. A _____ is a collection of symbols, experiences and associations connected with a product, a service, a person or any other artifact or entity.

   _____s have become increasingly important components of culture and the economy, now being described as 'cultural accessories and personal philosophies'.

   Some people distinguish the psychological aspect of a _____ from the experiential aspect.

   a. Brand
   b. Brand equity
   c. Store brand
   d. Brandable software

14. _____ is the application of marketing techniques to a specific product, product line, or brand. It seeks to increase the product's perceived value to the customer and thereby increase brand franchise and brand equity. Marketers see a brand as an implied promise that the level of quality people have come to expect from a brand will continue with future purchases of the same product.

   a. Store brand
   b. Trademark distinctiveness
   c. Naming rights
   d. Brand management

15. _____ is a service provided by many retailers of various products, primarily electronics, that provides the end-user with a resource for information regarding the product, and help if the product should malfunction. _____ can be found in most manuals for products in the form of a phone number, website address, or physical location.

   The Internet has allowed for a new form of _____ to develop.

   a. Psychological pricing
   b. Product life cycle
   c. Price-weighted
   d. Product support

16. In economics, business, retail, and accounting, a _____ is the value of money that has been used up to produce something, and hence is not available for use anymore. In economics, a _____ is an alternative that is given up as a result of a decision. In business, the _____ may be one of acquisition, in which case the amount of money expended to acquire it is counted as _____.

Chapter 13. Designing and Managing Services

a. Transaction cost
b. Variable cost
c. Fixed costs
d. Cost

17. An _____ is quite usually a standard guarantee from the seller of a product that specifies the extent to which the quality or performance of the product is assured and states the conditions under which the product can be returned, replaced, or repaired. It is often given in the form of a specific, written 'Warranty' document. However, a warranty may also arise by operation of law based upon the seller's description of the goods, and perhaps their source and quality, and any material deviation from that specification would violate the guarantee.

a. Express warranty
b. Imperial Group v. Philip Morris
c. Energy Star
d. Office for Harmonization in the Internal Market

Chapter 14. Developing Pricing Strategies and Programs

1. _____ is one of the four Ps of the marketing mix. The other three aspects are product, promotion, and place. It is also a key variable in microeconomic price allocation theory.
   a. Competitor indexing
   b. Pricing
   c. Relationship based pricing
   d. Price

2. Electronic commerce, commonly known as _____ or eCommerce, consists of the buying and selling of products or services over electronic systems such as the Internet and other computer networks. The amount of trade conducted electronically has grown extraordinarily with wide-spread Internet usage. A wide variety of commerce is conducted in this way, spurring and drawing on innovations in electronic funds transfer, supply chain management, Internet marketing, online transaction processing, electronic data interchange (EDI), inventory management systems, and automated data collection systems.
   a. AMAX
   b. ADTECH
   c. ACNielsen
   d. E-commerce

3. _____ is a broad label that refers to any individuals or households that use goods and services generated within the economy. The concept of a _____ is used in different contexts, so that the usage and significance of the term may vary.

A _____ is a person who uses any product or service.

   a. 6-3-5 Brainwriting
   b. Consumer
   c. Power III
   d. 180SearchAssistant

4. _____ in economics and business is the result of an exchange and from that trade we assign a numerical monetary value to a good, service or asset. If I trade 4 apples for an orange, the _____ of an orange is 4 - apples. Inversely, the _____ of an apple is 1/4 oranges.
   a. Price
   b. Discounts and allowances
   c. Pricing
   d. Contribution margin-based pricing

5. In economics, _____ is the desire to own something and the ability to pay for it. The term _____ signifies the ability or the willingness to buy a particular commodity at a given point of time.

   a. Market system
   b. Discretionary spending
   c. Market dominance
   d. Demand

6. _____ are prices at which demand is relatively high. In introductory microeconomics, a demand curve is downward sloping to the right and either linear or gently convex to the origin. The first is usually true, but the second is only piecewise true, as price surveys indicate that demand for a product is not a linear function of its price and not even a smooth function.
   a. Relationship based pricing
   b. Price markdown
   c. Fee
   d. Price points

7. In economics, _____ is the ratio of the percent change in one variable to the percent change in another variable. It is a tool for measuring the responsiveness of a function to changes in parameters in a relative way. Commonly analyzed are _____ of substitution, price and wealth.

Chapter 14. Developing Pricing Strategies and Programs

   a. Intellectual property
   b. ACNielsen
   c. Opinion leadership
   d. Elasticity

8. Price _____ is defined as the measure of responsiveness in the quantity demanded for a commodity as a result of change in price of the same commodity. It is a measure of how consumers react to a change in price. In other words, it is percentage change in quantity demanded as per the percentage change in price of the same commodity.
   a. ADTECH
   b. ACNielsen
   c. Elasticity of Demand
   d. AMAX

9. _____ is defined as the measure of responsiveness in the quantity demanded for a commodity as a result of change in price of the same commodity. It is a measure of how consumers react to a change in price. In other words, it is percentage change in quantity demanded as per the percentage change in price of the same commodity.
   a. Power III
   b. 6-3-5 Brainwriting
   c. 180SearchAssistant
   d. Price elasticity of Demand

10. In economics, business, retail, and accounting, a _____ is the value of money that has been used up to produce something, and hence is not available for use anymore. In economics, a _____ is an alternative that is given up as a result of a decision. In business, the _____ may be one of acquisition, in which case the amount of money expended to acquire it is counted as _____.
   a. Variable cost
   b. Fixed costs
   c. Cost
   d. Transaction cost

11. In economics, _____ are business expenses that are not dependent on the activities of the business They tend to be time-related, such as salaries or rents being paid per month. This is in contrast to variable costs, which are volume-related (and are paid per quantity.)

In management accounting, _____ are defined as expenses that do not change in proportion to the activity of a business, within the relevant period or scale of production.

   a. Variable cost
   b. Transaction cost
   c. Marginal cost
   d. Fixed costs

12. _____s are used in open sentences. For instance, in the formula x + 1 = 5, x is a _____ which represents an 'unknown' number. _____s are often represented by letters of the Roman alphabet, or those of other alphabets, such as Greek, and use other special symbols.
   a. Book of business
   b. Quantitative
   c. Variable
   d. Personalization

13. _____s are expenses that change in proportion to the activity of a business. In other words, _____ is the sum of marginal costs. It can also be considered normal costs.
   a. Transaction cost
   b. Marginal cost
   c. Fixed costs
   d. Variable cost

14. A _____ is a plan of action designed to achieve a particular goal.

Chapter 14. Developing Pricing Strategies and Programs 71

_____ is different from tactics. In military terms, tactics is concerned with the conduct of an engagement while _____ is concerned with how different engagements are linked.

a. Power III
b. 180SearchAssistant
c. 6-3-5 Brainwriting
d. Strategy

15. In mathematics, an _____, or central tendency of a data set refers to a measure of the 'middle' or 'expected' value of the data set. There are many different descriptive statistics that can be chosen as a measurement of the central tendency of the data items.

An _____ is a single value that is meant to typify a list of values.

a. ACNielsen
b. Average
c. AMAX
d. ADTECH

16. In economics, _____ is equal to total cost divided by the number of goods produced (the output quantity, Q.) It is also equal to the sum of average variable costs (total variable costs divided by Q) plus average fixed costs (total fixed costs divided by Q.) _____s may be dependent on the time period considered (increasing production may be expensive or impossible in the short term, for example.)

a. ACNielsen
b. Average cost
c. ADTECH
d. Average variable cost

17. In economics, and cost accounting, _____ describes the total economic cost of production and is made up of variable costs, which vary according to the quantity of a good produced and include inputs such as labor and raw materials, plus fixed costs, which are independent of the quantity of a good produced and include inputs (capital) that cannot be varied in the short term, such as buildings and machinery. _____ in economics includes the total opportunity cost of each factor of production in addition to fixed and variable costs.

The rate at which _____ changes as the amount produced changes is called marginal cost.

a. Product proliferation
b. Household production function
c. Total cost
d. Hoarding

18. _____ is a pricing method used by firms. It is defined as 'a cost management tool for reducing the overall cost of a product over its entire life-cycle with the help of production, engineering, research and design'. _____ finds the maximum amount of cost that can be incurred on a product and with it the firm can still earn the required profit margin from that product at a particular selling price.

a. Premium pricing
b. Fee
c. Competitor indexing
d. Target costing

19. A personal and cultural _____ is a relative ethic _____, an assumption upon which implementation can be extrapolated. A _____ system is a set of consistent _____s and measures that is soo not true. A principle _____ is a foundation upon which other _____s and measures of integrity are based.

Chapter 14. Developing Pricing Strategies and Programs

a. Supreme Court of the United States
b. Package-on-Package
c. Perceptual maps
d. Value

20. _____, in marketing, is the practice of modifying a basic list price based on the geographical location of the buyer. It is intended to reflect the costs of shipping to different locations.

There are several types of geographic pricing:

- FOB origin (Free on Board origin) - The shipping cost from the factory or warehouse is paid by the purchaser. Ownership of the goods is transferred to the buyer as soon as it leaves the point of origin. It can be either the buyer or seller that arranges for the transportation.
- Uniform delivery pricing - (also called postage stamp pricing) - The same price is charged to all.
- Zone pricing - Prices increase as shipping distances increase. This is sometimes done by drawing concentric circles on a map with the plant or warehouse at the center and each circle defining the boundary of a price zone. Instead of using circles, irregularly shaped price boundaries can be drawn that reflect geography, population density, transportation infrastructure, and shipping cost. (The term 'zone pricing' can also refer to the practice of setting prices that reflect local competitive conditions, i.e., the market forces of supply and demand, rather than actual cost of transportation.)

Zone pricing, as practiced in the gasoline industry in the United States, is the pricing of gasoline based on a complex and secret weighting of factors, such as the number of competing stations, number of vehicles, average traffic flow, population density, and geographic characteristics. This can result in two branded gas stations only a few miles apart selling gasoline at a price differential of as much as $0.50 per gallon.

a. Green market
b. Countervailing duties
c. Geographical pricing
d. Competitive

21. _____ is exchanging goods or services that are paid for, in whole or part, with other goods or services.

There are five main variants of _____:

- Barter: Exchange of goods or services directly for other goods or services without the use of money as means of purchase or payment.
- Switch trading: Practice in which one company sells to another its obligation to make a purchase in a given country.
- Counter purchase: Sale of goods and services to a country by a company that promises to make a future purchase of a specific product from the country.
- Buyback: occurs when a firm builds a plant in a country - or supplies technology, equipment, training, or other services to the country and agrees to take a certain percentage of the plant's output as partial payment for the contract.
- Offset: Agreement that a company will offset a hard - currency purchase of an unspecified product from that nation in the future. Agreement by one nation to buy a product from another, subject to the purchase of some or all of the components and raw materials from the buyer of the finished product, or the assembly of such product in the buyer nation.

Chapter 14. Developing Pricing Strategies and Programs

a. RFM
b. Merchant
c. Retail loss prevention
d. Countertrade

22. _____ are reductions to a basic price of goods or services. They can occur anywhere in the distribution channel, modifying either the manufacturer's list price (determined by the manufacturer and often printed on the package), the retail price (set by the retailer and often attached to the product with a sticker), or the list price (which is quoted to a potential buyer, usually in written form.) The market price (also called effective price) is the amount actually paid.

a. Price
b. Discounts and allowances
c. Price points
d. Price shading

23. _____ exists when sales of identical goods or services are transacted at different prices from the same provider. In a theoretical market with perfect information, no transaction costs or prohibition on secondary exchange (or re-selling) to prevent arbitrage, _____ can only be a feature of monopoly and oligopoly markets, where market power can be exercised. Otherwise, the moment the seller tries to sell the same good at different prices, the buyer at the lower price can arbitrage by selling to the consumer buying at the higher price but with a tiny discount.

a. Penetration pricing
b. Resale price maintenance
c. Price
d. Price discrimination

Chapter 15. Designing and Managing Value Networks and Channels

1. _____ is defined by the American _____ Association as the activity, set of institutions, and processes for creating, communicating, delivering, and exchanging offerings that have value for customers, clients, partners, and society at large. The term developed from the original meaning which referred literally to going to market, as in shopping, or going to a market to sell goods or services.

_____ practice tends to be seen as a creative industry, which includes advertising, distribution and selling.

   a. Marketing
   c. Customer acquisition management
   b. Product naming
   d. Marketing myopia

2. The business terms _____ and pull originated in the logistic and supply chain management, but are also widely used in marketing.

A _____-pull-system in business describes the move of a product or information between two subjects. On markets the consumers usually 'pulls' the goods or information they demand for their needs, while the offerers or suppliers '_____es' them toward the consumers.

   a. Push
   c. Manufacturers' representatives
   b. Completely randomized designs
   d. Gold Key Matching Service

3. A _____ is a plan of action designed to achieve a particular goal.

_____ is different from tactics. In military terms, tactics is concerned with the conduct of an engagement while _____ is concerned with how different engagements are linked.

   a. Strategy
   c. 6-3-5 Brainwriting
   b. Power III
   d. 180SearchAssistant

4. In economics, _____ is the desire to own something and the ability to pay for it. The term _____ signifies the ability or the willingness to buy a particular commodity at a given point of time.

   a. Market dominance
   c. Demand
   b. Market system
   d. Discretionary spending

5. A personal and cultural _____ is a relative ethic _____, an assumption upon which implementation can be extrapolated. A _____ system is a set of consistent _____s and measures that is soo not true. A principle _____ is a foundation upon which other _____s and measures of integrity are based.
   a. Package-on-Package
   c. Perceptual maps
   b. Supreme Court of the United States
   d. Value

6. A _____ is a complex set of social and technical resources. _____s work together via relationships to create social goods (public goods) or economic value.

This value takes the form of knowledge and other intangibles and/or financial value.

Chapter 15. Designing and Managing Value Networks and Channels

a. 180SearchAssistant
b. Power III
c. Value network
d. 6-3-5 Brainwriting

7. _____ in organizations and public policy is both the organizational process of creating and maintaining a plan; and the psychological process of thinking about the activities required to create a desired goal on some scale. As such, it is a fundamental property of intelligent behavior. This thought process is essential to the creation and refinement of a plan, or integration of it with other plans, that is, it combines forecasting of developments with the preparation of scenarios of how to react to them.

a. 180SearchAssistant
b. 6-3-5 Brainwriting
c. Power III
d. Planning

8. A _____ is a list of the general tasks and responsibilities of a position. Typically, it also includes to whom the position reports, specifications such as the qualifications needed by the person in the job, salary range for the position, etc. A _____ is usually developed by conducting a job analysis, which includes examining the tasks and sequences of tasks necessary to perform the job.

a. 180SearchAssistant
b. Power III
c. 6-3-5 Brainwriting
d. Job description

9. _____ is an advertisement in which a particular product specifically mentions a competitor by name for the express purpose of showing why the competitor is inferior to the product naming it.

This should not be confused with parody advertisements, where a fictional product is being advertised for the purpose of poking fun at the particular advertisement, nor should it be confused with the use of a coined brand name for the purpose of comparing the product without actually naming an actual competitor. ('Wikipedia tastes better and is less filling than the Encyclopedia Galactica.')

In the 1980s, during what has been referred to as the cola wars, soft-drink manufacturer Pepsi ran a series of advertisements where people, caught on hidden camera, in a blind taste test, chose Pepsi over rival Coca-Cola.

a. Cost per conversion
b. GL-70
c. Heavy-up
d. Comparative advertising

10. The _____ is one of the three economic sectors, the others being the secondary sector and the primary sector The general definition of the Tertiary sector is producing a service instead of just a end product, in the case of the secondary sector. Sometimes an additional sector, the 'quaternary sector', is defined for the sharing of information

a. 180SearchAssistant
b. Power III
c. 6-3-5 Brainwriting
d. Tertiary sector of economy

11. _____ is one of the four elements of marketing mix. An organization or set of organizations (go-betweens) involved in the process of making a product or service available for use or consumption by a consumer or business user.

The other three parts of the marketing mix are product, pricing, and promotion.

a. Distribution
b. Japan Advertising Photographers' Association
c. Comparison-Shopping agent
d. Better Living Through Chemistry

Chapter 15. Designing and Managing Value Networks and Channels

12. _____ occurs when manufacturers (brands) disintermediate their channel partners, such as distributors, retailers, dealers, and sales representatives, by selling their products direct to consumers through general marketing methods and/or over the internet through eCommerce.

Some manufacturers want their brands to capture the power of the internet but do not want to create conflict with their other distribution channels, as these partners are necessary and viable for any manufacturer to maintain and gain success. The Census Bureau of the U.S. Department of Commerce reported that online sales in 2005 grew 24.6 percent over 2004 to reach 86.3 billion dollars.

a. Trade Symbols
b. Channel conflict
c. Store brand
d. Retail design

13. _____ is a rivalry between individuals, groups, nations for territory, a niche, or allocation of resources. It arises whenever two or more parties strive for a goal which cannot be shared. _____ occurs naturally between living organisms which co-exist in the same environment.

a. Price fixing
b. Competition
c. Price competition
d. Non-price competition

14. Electronic commerce, commonly known as _____ or eCommerce, consists of the buying and selling of products or services over electronic systems such as the Internet and other computer networks. The amount of trade conducted electronically has grown extraordinarily with wide-spread Internet usage. A wide variety of commerce is conducted in this way, spurring and drawing on innovations in electronic funds transfer, supply chain management, Internet marketing, online transaction processing, electronic data interchange (EDI), inventory management systems, and automated data collection systems.

a. E-commerce
b. ADTECH
c. ACNielsen
d. AMAX

15. _____ is a term commonly used to describe commerce transactions between businesses like the one between a manufacturer and a wholesaler or a wholesaler and a retailer i.e both the buyer and the seller are business entity.This is unlike business-to-consumers (B2C) which involve a business entity and end consumer, or business-to-government (B2G) which involve a business entity and government.

The volume of B2B transactions is much higher than the volume of B2C transactions. The primary reason for this is that in a typical supply chain there will be many B2B transactions involving subcomponent or raw materials, and only one B2C transaction, specifically sale of the finished product to the end customer.

a. Social marketing
b. Disruptive technology
c. Customer relationship management
d. Business-to-business

Chapter 16. Managing Retailing, Wholesaling, and Logistics

1. _____ consists of the sale of goods or merchandise from a fixed location, such as a department store or kiosk in small or individual lots for direct consumption by the purchaser. _____ may include subordinated services, such as delivery. Purchasers may be individuals or businesses.
   a. Warehouse store
   b. Retailing
   c. Thrifting
   d. Charity shop

2. _____ is an advertisement in which a particular product specifically mentions a competitor by name for the express purpose of showing why the competitor is inferior to the product naming it.

This should not be confused with parody advertisements, where a fictional product is being advertised for the purpose of poking fun at the particular advertisement, nor should it be confused with the use of a coined brand name for the purpose of comparing the product without actually naming an actual competitor. ('Wikipedia tastes better and is less filling than the Encyclopedia Galactica.')

In the 1980s, during what has been referred to as the cola wars, soft-drink manufacturer Pepsi ran a series of advertisements where people, caught on hidden camera, in a blind taste test, chose Pepsi over rival Coca-Cola.

   a. Cost per conversion
   b. Heavy-up
   c. Comparative advertising
   d. GL-70

3. _____ is a retailing concept in which the total range of products sold by a retailer is broken down into discrete groups of similar or related products; these groups are known as product categories. Examples of grocery categories may be: tinned fish, washing detergent, toothpastes, etc. Each category is then run like a 'mini business' (Business Unit) in its own right, with its own set of turnover and/or profitability targets and strategies. An important facet of _____ is the shift in relationship between retailer and supplier : instead of the traditional adversarial relationship, the relationship moves to one of collaboration, exchange of information and data and joint business building. The focus of all negotiations is centered around the effects of the turnover of the total category, not just the sales on the individual products therein.
   a. Brochure
   b. Market segment
   c. Societal marketing
   d. Category management

4. A _____ is a retail establishment which specializes in selling a wide range of products without a single predominant merchandise line. _____s usually sell products including apparel, furniture, appliances, electronics, and additionally select other lines of products such as paint, hardware, toiletries, cosmetics, photographic equipment, jewelery, toys, and sporting goods. Certain _____s are further classified as discount _____s.
   a. 6-3-5 Brainwriting
   b. Power III
   c. Department store
   d. 180SearchAssistant

5. _____ is a sub-discipline and type of marketing. There are two main definitional characteristics which distinguish it from other types of marketing. The first is that it attempts to send its messages directly to consumers, without the use of intervening media.
   a. Direct marketing
   b. Database marketing
   c. Direct Marketing Associations
   d. Power III

6. _____ is a retail channel for the distribution of goods and services. At a basic level it may be defined as marketing and selling products, direct to consumers away from a fixed retail location. Sales are typically made through party plan, one to one demonstrations, and other personal contact arrangements.

a. 180SearchAssistant
b. 6-3-5 Brainwriting
c. Direct selling
d. Power III

7. _____, is a form of Network Marketing (however the terms are often used interchangeably.) It is a marketing strategy that compensates promoters of direct selling companies not only for product sales they personally generate, but also for the sales of others they introduced to the company. The products and company are usually marketed directly to consumers and potential business partners by means of relationship referrals and word of mouth marketing.
   a. Multi-level marketing
   b. Service provider
   c. Pay to surf
   d. Cross-selling

8. _____ is a method of direct marketing in which a salesperson solicits to prospective customers to buy products or services, either over the phone or through a subsequent face to face or Web conferencing appointment scheduled during the call.

_____ can also include recorded sales pitches programmed to be played over the phone via automatic dialing. _____ has come under fire in recent years, being viewed as an annoyance by many.

   a. Phishing
   b. Joe job
   c. Directory Harvest Attack
   d. Telemarketing

9. _____ is defined by the American _____ Association as the activity, set of institutions, and processes for creating, communicating, delivering, and exchanging offerings that have value for customers, clients, partners, and society at large. The term developed from the original meaning which referred literally to going to market, as in shopping, or going to a market to sell goods or services.

_____ practice tends to be seen as a creative industry, which includes advertising, distribution and selling.

   a. Product naming
   b. Marketing myopia
   c. Marketing
   d. Customer acquisition management

10. _____ is the examining of goods or services from retailers with the intent to purchase at that time. _____ is an activity of selection and/or purchase. In some contexts it is considered a leisure activity as well as an economic one.
    a. Discount store
    b. Khodebshchik
    c. Hawkers
    d. Shopping

11. _____ refers to the methods of practicing and using another person's philosophy of business. The franchisor grants the independent operator the right to distribute its products, techniques, and trademarks for a percentage of gross monthly sales and a royalty fee. Various tangibles and intangibles such as national or international advertising, training, and other support services are commonly made available by the franchisor.
    a. Power III
    b. Franchise fee
    c. 180SearchAssistant
    d. Franchising

12. _____ is the use of an object (typically referred to as an RFID tag) applied to or incorporated into a product, animal, or person for the purpose of identification and tracking using radio waves. Some tags can be read from several meters away and beyond the line of sight of the reader.

Most RFID tags contain at least two parts.

a. 180SearchAssistant
b. Power III
c. Radio-frequency identification
d. 6-3-5 Brainwriting

13. _____ in economics and business is the result of an exchange and from that trade we assign a numerical monetary value to a good, service or asset. If I trade 4 apples for an orange, the _____ of an orange is 4 - apples. Inversely, the _____ of an apple is 1/4 oranges.

a. Contribution margin-based pricing
b. Discounts and allowances
c. Pricing
d. Price

14. In marketing, _____ has come to mean the process by which marketers try to create an image or identity in the minds of their target market for its product, brand, or organization. It is the 'relative competitive comparison' their product occupies in a given market as perceived by the target market.

Re-_____ involves changing the identity of a product, relative to the identity of competing products, in the collective minds of the target market.

a. GE matrix
b. Containerization
c. Moratorium
d. Positioning

15. _____ is one of the four Ps of the marketing mix. The other three aspects are product, promotion, and place. It is also a key variable in microeconomic price allocation theory.

a. Relationship based pricing
b. Price
c. Pricing
d. Competitor indexing

16. A _____ is a large outdoor advertising structure (a billing board), typically found in high traffic areas such as alongside busy roads. _____s present large advertisements to passing pedestrians and drivers. Typically showing large, ostensibly witty slogans, and distinctive visuals, _____s are highly visible in the top designated market areas.

a. Billboard
b. Power III
c. 6-3-5 Brainwriting
d. 180SearchAssistant

17. A _____ is a collection of symbols, experiences and associations connected with a product, a service, a person or any other artifact or entity.

_____s have become increasingly important components of culture and the economy, now being described as 'cultural accessories and personal philosophies'.

Some people distinguish the psychological aspect of a _____ from the experiential aspect.

a. Brand equity
b. Brandable software
c. Store brand
d. Brand

Chapter 16. Managing Retailing, Wholesaling, and Logistics

18. _____ is the management of the flow of goods, information and other resources, including energy and people, between the point of origin and the point of consumption in order to meet the requirements of consumers (frequently, and originally, military organizations.) _____ involves the integration of information, transportation, inventory, warehousing, material-handling, and packaging. _____ is a channel of the supply chain which adds the value of time and place utility.

a. Logistics
b. Power III
c. 180SearchAssistant
d. 6-3-5 Brainwriting

19. _____ is a list for goods and materials held available in stock by a business. It is also used for a list of the contents of a household and for a list for testamentary purposes of the possessions of someone who has died. In accounting _____ is considered an asset.

a. ADTECH
b. Inventory
c. Ending Inventory
d. ACNielsen

20. _____ is a system of intermodal freight transport using standard intermodal containers that are standardised by the International Organization for Standardization (ISO.) These can be loaded and sealed intact onto container ships, railroad cars, planes, and trucks.

a. BeyondROI
b. Rebate
c. Scientific controls
d. Containerization

Chapter 17. Designing and Managing Integrated Marketing Communications

1. A _____ is a collection of symbols, experiences and associations connected with a product, a service, a person or any other artifact or entity.

_____s have become increasingly important components of culture and the economy, now being described as 'cultural accessories and personal philosophies'.

Some people distinguish the psychological aspect of a _____ from the experiential aspect.

   a. Brand equity
   c. Store brand
   b. Brandable software
   d. Brand

2. _____ refers to the marketing effects or outcomes that accrue to a product with its brand name compared with those that would accrue if the same product did not have the brand name . And, at the root of these marketing effects is consumers' knowledge. In other words, consumers' knowledge about a brand makes manufacturers/advertisers respond differently or adopt appropriately adapt measures for the marketing of the brand .
   a. Brand aversion
   c. Product extension
   b. Brand equity
   d. Brand image

3. _____ is defined by the American _____ Association as the activity, set of institutions, and processes for creating, communicating, delivering, and exchanging offerings that have value for customers, clients, partners, and society at large. The term developed from the original meaning which referred literally to going to market, as in shopping, or going to a market to sell goods or services.

_____ practice tends to be seen as a creative industry, which includes advertising, distribution and selling.

   a. Product naming
   c. Customer acquisition management
   b. Marketing myopia
   d. Marketing

4. _____ refers to messages and related media used to communicate with a market. Those who practice advertising, branding, direct marketing, graphic design, marketing, packaging, promotion, publicity, sponsorship, public relations, sales, sales promotion and online marketing are termed marketing communicators, _____ managers, or more briefly as marcom managers.
   a. Merchandising
   c. Sales promotion
   b. Merchandise
   d. Marketing communication

5. In marketing and advertising, a _____ usually an advertising campaign, is aimed at appealing to. A _____ can be people of a certain age group, gender, marital status, etc. (ex: teenagers, females, single people, etc.)
   a. Targeted advertising
   c. National brand
   b. Brand Development Index
   d. Target audience

6. _____ is a marketing concept that refers to a consumer knowing of a brand's existence; at aggregate (brand) level it refers to the proportion of consumers who know of the brand.

Chapter 17. Designing and Managing Integrated Marketing Communications

_____ can be measured by showing a consumer the brand and asking whether or not they knew of it beforehand. However, in common market research practice a variety of recognition and recall measures of _____ are employed all of which test the brand name's association to a product category cue, this came about because most market research in the 20th Century was conducted by post or telephone, actually showing the brand to consumers usually required more expensive face-to-face interviews (until web-based interviews became possible.)

    a. Fitting Group
    c. Brand orientation
    b. Brand equity
    d. Brand awareness

7. The term _____, invented to replace the older gender-based terms, is a typical example of a gender-neutral neologism.

In the present media-sensitive world, many organizations are increasingly likely to employ professionals who have received formal training in journalism, communications, public relations and public affairs in this role in order to ensure that public announcements are made in the most appropriate fashion and through the most appropriate channels to maximize the impact of favorable messages, and to minimize the impact of unfavorable messages. Popular local and national sports stars are often chosen as spokespeople for commercial advertising.

    a. Professional services
    c. Spokesperson
    b. Power III
    d. 180SearchAssistant

8. _____ or simply buzz is a term used in word-of-mouth marketing. The interaction of consumers and users of a product or service serve to amplify the original marketing message.

Some describe buzz as a form of hype among consumers, a vague but positive association, excitement, or anticipation about a product or service.

    a. Multidimensional scaling
    c. Consumption smoothing
    b. Consumer confidence
    d. Marketing buzz

9. _____ and viral advertising refer to marketing techniques that use pre-existing social networks to produce increases in brand awareness or to achieve other marketing objectives (such as product sales) through self-replicating viral processes, analogous to the spread of pathological and computer viruses. It can be word-of-mouth delivered or enhanced by the network effects of the Internet. Viral promotions may take the form of video clips, interactive Flash games, advergames, ebooks, brandable software, images, or even text messages.

    a. New Media Marketing
    c. 180SearchAssistant
    b. Viral marketing
    d. Power III

10. A _____ is a brief statement of the purpose of a company, organization. It is ideally used to guide the actions of the organization.

Chapter 17. Designing and Managing Integrated Marketing Communications 83

_____s often contain the following:

- Purpose of the organization
- The organization's primary stakeholders: clients, stockholders, etc.
- Responsibilities of the organization towards these stockholders
- Products and services offered

Generally shorter _____s are more effective than longer ones.

In developing a _____:

- Encourage input as feasible from employees, volunteers, and other stakeholders
- Publicize it broadly

The _____ can be used to resolve differences between business stakeholders. Stakeholders include: employees including managers and executives, stockholders, board of directors, customers, suppliers, distributors, creditors, governments (local, state, federal, etc.), unions, competitors, NGO's, and the general public.

    a. 6-3-5 Brainwriting   b. Mission statement
    c. 180SearchAssistant   d. Power III

11. _____ generally refers to a list of all planned expenses and revenues. It is a plan for saving and spending. A _____ is an important concept in microeconomics, which uses a _____ line to illustrate the trade-offs between two or more goods.
    a. Budget   b. Power III
    c. 6-3-5 Brainwriting   d. 180SearchAssistant

12. _____ is a form of communication that typically attempts to persuade potential customers to purchase or to consume more of a particular brand of product or service. 'While now central to the contemporary global economy and the reproduction of global production networks, it is only quite recently that _____ has been more than a marginal influence on patterns of sales and production. The formation of modern _____ was intimately bound up with the emergence of new forms of monopoly capitalism around the end of the 19th and beginning of the 20th century as one element in corporate strategies to create, organize and where possible control markets, especially for mass produced consumer goods.
    a. Advertising   b. ACNielsen
    c. AMAX   d. ADTECH

13. _____ is the practice of managing the flow of information between an organization and its publics. _____ - often referred to as _____ - gains an organization or individual exposure to their audiences using topics of public interest and news items that do not require direct payment. Because _____ places exposure in credible third-party outlets, it offers a third-party legitimacy that advertising does not have.
    a. Graphic communication   b. Power III
    c. Public relations   d. Symbolic analysis

Chapter 17. Designing and Managing Integrated Marketing Communications

14. _____ is the deliberate attempt to manage the public's perception of a subject. The subjects of _____ include people (for example, politicians and performing artists), goods and services, organizations of all kinds, and works of art or entertainment.

From a marketing perspective, _____ is one component of promotion.

  a. Publicity
  b. Brando
  c. Little value placed on potential benefits
  d. Pearson's chi-square

15. _____ is one of the four aspects of promotional mix. (The other three parts of the promotional mix are advertising, personal selling, and publicity/public relations.) Media and non-media marketing communication are employed for a pre-determined, limited time to increase consumer demand, stimulate market demand or improve product availability.

  a. Merchandise
  b. New Media Strategies
  c. Marketing communication
  d. Sales promotion

16. _____ involves disseminating information about a product, product line, brand, or company. It is one of the four key aspects of the marketing mix. (The other three elements are product marketing, pricing, and distribution). P>_____ is generally sub-divided into two parts:

- Above the line _____: Promotion in the media (e.g. TV, radio, newspapers, Internet and Mobile Phones) in which the advertiser pays an advertising agency to place the ad
- Below the line _____: All other _____. Much of this is intended to be subtle enough for the consumer to be unaware that _____ is taking place. E.g. sponsorship, product placement, endorsements, sales _____, merchandising, direct mail, personal selling, public relations, trade shows

  a. Promotion
  b. Davie Brown Index
  c. Cashmere Agency
  d. Bottling lines

17. _____ is a sub-discipline and type of marketing. There are two main definitional characteristics which distinguish it from other types of marketing. The first is that it attempts to send its messages directly to consumers, without the use of intervening media.

  a. Power III
  b. Database marketing
  c. Direct Marketing Associations
  d. Direct marketing

18. _____ , according to The American Marketing Association, is 'a planning process designed to assure that all brand contacts received by a customer or prospect for a product, service, or organization are relevant to that person and consistent over time.' (Marketing Power Dictionary)

_____ is a term used to describe a holistic approach to marketing. It aims to ensure consistency of message and the complementary use of media. The concept includes online and offline marketing channels.

  a. Integrated marketing communications
  b. ACNielsen
  c. ADTECH
  d. AMAX

19. In statistics, an _____ is a term in a statistical model added when the effect of two or more variables is not simply additive. Such a term reflects that the effect of one variable depends on the values of one or more other variables.

Thus, for a response Y and two variables x_1 and x_2 an additive model would be:

$$Y = ax_1 + bx_2 + \text{error}$$

In contrast to this,

$$Y = ax_1 + bx_2 + c(x_1 \times x_2) + \text{error},$$

is an example of a model with an _____ between variables x_1 and x_2 ('error' refers to the random variable whose value by which y differs from the expected value of y.)

a. AMAX
b. Interaction
c. ADTECH
d. ACNielsen

Chapter 18. Managing Mass Communications

1. _____ is a form of communication that typically attempts to persuade potential customers to purchase or to consume more of a particular brand of product or service. 'While now central to the contemporary global economy and the reproduction of global production networks, it is only quite recently that _____ has been more than a marginal influence on patterns of sales and production. The formation of modern _____ was intimately bound up with the emergence of new forms of monopoly capitalism around the end of the 19th and beginning of the 20th century as one element in corporate strategies to create, organize and where possible control markets, especially for mass produced consumer goods.

   a. ADTECH
   c. AMAX
   b. Advertising
   d. ACNielsen

2. _____ is when advertising is carried out in an informative manner Also, _____ tends to help generate a good reputation.

In some circumstances a business might be required to run _____ as part of resolving a law suit. Tobacco companies are one of the more notable examples of this.

   a. Out-of-home advertising
   c. ACNielsen
   b. ADTECH
   d. Informative advertising

3. _____ is a form of social influence. It is the process of guiding people toward the adoption of an idea, attitude, or action by rational and symbolic (though not always logical) means. It is strategy of problem-solving relying on 'appeals' rather than coercion.

   a. 180SearchAssistant
   c. Power III
   b. 6-3-5 Brainwriting
   d. Persuasion

4. In operant conditioning, _____ occurs when an event following a response causes an increase in the probability of that response occurring in the future. Response strength can be assessed by measures such as the frequency with which the response is made (for example, a pigeon may peck a key more times in the session), or the speed with which it is made (for example, a rat may run a maze faster.) The environment change contingent upon the response is called a reinforcer.

   a. Reinforcement
   c. Generic brands
   b. Completely randomized designs
   d. Relationship Management Application

5. _____ generally refers to a list of all planned expenses and revenues. It is a plan for saving and spending. A _____ is an important concept in microeconomics, which uses a _____ line to illustrate the trade-offs between two or more goods.

   a. 6-3-5 Brainwriting
   c. Power III
   b. 180SearchAssistant
   d. Budget

6. A _____ is a plan of action designed to achieve a particular goal.

_____ is different from tactics. In military terms, tactics is concerned with the conduct of an engagement while _____ is concerned with how different engagements are linked.

   a. Power III
   c. 6-3-5 Brainwriting
   b. 180SearchAssistant
   d. Strategy

7. _____ is a market coverage strategy in which a firm decides to ignore market segment differences and go after the whole market with one offer.it is type of marketing (or attempting to sell through persuasion) of a product to a wide audience. The idea is to broadcast a message that will reach the largest number of people possible. Traditionally _____ has focused on radio, television and newspapers as the medium used to reach this broad audience.
   a. Marketspace
   b. Cyberdoc
   c. Business-to-consumer
   d. Mass marketing

8. _____ is the term used to describe the academic study of the various means by which individuals and entities relay information through mass media to large segments of the population at the same time. It is usually understood to relate to newspaper and magazine publishing, radio, television and film, as these are used both for disseminating news and for advertising.

_____ research includes media institutions and processes such as diffusion of information, and media effects such as persuasion or manipulation of public opinion.

   a. Power III
   b. 6-3-5 Brainwriting
   c. 180SearchAssistant
   d. Mass communication

9. A _____ is a subgroup of people or organizations sharing one or more characteristics that cause them to have similar product and/or service needs. A true _____ meets all of the following criteria: it is distinct from other segments (different segments have different needs), it is homogeneous within the segment (exhibits common needs); it responds similarly to a market stimulus, and it can be reached by a market intervention. The term is also used when consumers with identical product and/or service needs are divided up into groups so they can be charged different amounts.
   a. Production orientation
   b. Customer insight
   c. Commercial planning
   d. Market segment

10. An _____ is an advertisement written in the form of an objective opinion editorial, and presented in a printed publication--usually designed to look like a legitimate and independent news story.

_____s differ from traditional advertisements in that they are designed to look like the articles that appear in the publication.

   a. ACNielsen
   b. Informative advertising
   c. Advertorial
   d. ADTECH

11. _____ is the combination of an audio-visual program and a brand. It can be initiated either by the brand or by the broadcaster.
   a. Brand image
   b. Brand loyalty
   c. Channel conflict
   d. Branded entertainment

12. _____ is a form of advertisement, where branded goods or services are placed in a context usually devoid of ads, such as movies, the story line of television shows Broadcasting ' Cable reported, 'Two thirds of advertisers employ 'branded entertainment'--_____--with the vast majority of that (80%) in commercial TV programming.' The story, based on a survey by the Association of National Advertisers, added, 'Reasons for using in-show plugs varied from 'stronger emotional connection' to better dovetailing with relevant content, to targetting a specific group.'

Chapter 18. Managing Mass Communications

_____ became common in the 1980s, but can be traced back to the nineteenth century in publishing.

a. 6-3-5 Brainwriting
b. Product placement
c. Power III
d. 180SearchAssistant

13. _____ are media (newspapers, radio, television, movies, Internet, etc.) which are alternatives to the business or government-owned mass media. Proponents of _____ argue that the mainstream media are biased.
  a. Alternative media
  b. AMAX
  c. ACNielsen
  d. ADTECH

14. _____ is one of the four aspects of promotional mix. (The other three parts of the promotional mix are advertising, personal selling, and publicity/public relations.) Media and non-media marketing communication are employed for a pre-determined, limited time to increase consumer demand, stimulate market demand or improve product availability.
  a. Marketing communication
  b. Merchandise
  c. New Media Strategies
  d. Sales promotion

15. In economics, _____ is the desire to own something and the ability to pay for it. The term _____ signifies the ability or the willingness to buy a particular commodity at a given point of time .

  a. Market dominance
  b. Discretionary spending
  c. Market system
  d. Demand

16. _____ involves disseminating information about a product, product line, brand, or company. It is one of the four key aspects of the marketing mix. (The other three elements are product marketing, pricing, and distribution). P>_____ is generally sub-divided into two parts:

  - Above the line _____: Promotion in the media (e.g. TV, radio, newspapers, Internet and Mobile Phones) in which the advertiser pays an advertising agency to place the ad
  - Below the line _____: All other _____. Much of this is intended to be subtle enough for the consumer to be unaware that _____ is taking place. E.g. sponsorship, product placement, endorsements, sales _____, merchandising, direct mail, personal selling, public relations, trade shows

  a. Bottling lines
  b. Davie Brown Index
  c. Cashmere Agency
  d. Promotion

17. _____ is the practice of influencing decisions made by government. It includes all attempts to influence legislators and officials, whether by other legislators, constituents or organized groups. A lobbyist is a person who tries to influence legislation on behalf of a special interest or a member of a lobby.
  a. Albert Einstein
  b. AStore
  c. African Americans
  d. Lobbying

Chapter 18. Managing Mass Communications

18. _____ is defined by the American _____ Association as the activity, set of institutions, and processes for creating, communicating, delivering, and exchanging offerings that have value for customers, clients, partners, and society at large. The term developed from the original meaning which referred literally to going to market, as in shopping, or going to a market to sell goods or services.

_____ practice tends to be seen as a creative industry, which includes advertising, distribution and selling.

a. Product naming
b. Marketing
c. Marketing myopia
d. Customer acquisition management

19. _____ is the practice of managing the flow of information between an organization and its publics. _____ - often referred to as _____ - gains an organization or individual exposure to their audiences using topics of public interest and news items that do not require direct payment. Because _____ places exposure in credible third-party outlets, it offers a third-party legitimacy that advertising does not have.

a. Public relations
b. Symbolic analysis
c. Power III
d. Graphic communication

20. _____ is the deliberate attempt to manage the public's perception of a subject. The subjects of _____ include people (for example, politicians and performing artists), goods and services, organizations of all kinds, and works of art or entertainment.

From a marketing perspective, _____ is one component of promotion.

a. Pearson's chi-square
b. Little value placed on potential benefits
c. Brando
d. Publicity

Chapter 19. Managing Personal Communications

1. _____ is a sub-discipline and type of marketing. There are two main definitional characteristics which distinguish it from other types of marketing. The first is that it attempts to send its messages directly to consumers, without the use of intervening media.
   a. Power III
   b. Database marketing
   c. Direct marketing
   d. Direct Marketing Associations

2. _____ is defined by the American _____ Association as the activity, set of institutions, and processes for creating, communicating, delivering, and exchanging offerings that have value for customers, clients, partners, and society at large. The term developed from the original meaning which referred literally to going to market, as in shopping, or going to a market to sell goods or services.

   _____ practice tends to be seen as a creative industry, which includes advertising, distribution and selling.

   a. Customer acquisition management
   b. Marketing
   c. Product naming
   d. Marketing myopia

3. Advertising mail junk mail is the delivery of advertising material to recipients of postal mail. The delivery of advertising mail forms a large and growing service for many postal services, and _____ marketing forms a significant portion of the direct marketing industry. Some organizations attempt to help people opt-out of receiving advertising mail, in many cases motivated by a concern over its negative environmental impact.
   a. Phishing
   b. Directory Harvest Attack
   c. Telemarketing
   d. Direct mail

4. _____ is a branch of philosophy which seeks to address questions about morality, such as how a moral outcome can be achieved in a specific situation (applied _____), how moral values should be determined (normative _____), what moral values people actually abide by (descriptive _____), what the fundamental semantic, ontological, and epistemic nature of _____ or morality is (meta-_____), and how moral capacity or moral agency develops and what its nature is (moral psychology.)

   Socrates was one of the first Greek philosophers to encourage both scholars and the common citizen to turn their attention from the outside world to the condition of man. In this view, Knowledge having a bearing on human life was placed highest, all other knowledge being secondary.

   a. AMAX
   b. ACNielsen
   c. Ethics
   d. ADTECH

5. A _____ is a structured collection of records or data that is stored in a computer system. The structure is achieved by organizing the data according to a _____ model. The model in most common use today is the relational model.
   a. 180SearchAssistant
   b. Power III
   c. 6-3-5 Brainwriting
   d. Database

6. _____ is a form of direct marketing using databases of customers or potential customers to generate personalized communications in order to promote a product or service for marketing purposes. The method of communication can be any addressable medium, as in direct marketing.

   The distinction between direct and _____ stems primarily from the attention paid to the analysis of data.

Chapter 19. Managing Personal Communications

a. Direct Marketing Associations
b. Database marketing
c. Direct marketing
d. Power III

7. _____ refers to the evolving trend in marketing whereby marketing has moved from a transaction-based effort to a conversation. The definition of _____ comes from John Deighton at Harvard, who says _____ is the ability to address the customer, remember what the customer says and address the customer again in a way that illustrates that we remember what the customer has told us (Deighton 1996.) _____ is not synonymous with online marketing, although _____ processes are facilitated by internet technology.
   a. European Information Technology Observatory
   b. InfoNU
   c. Outsourcing relationship management
   d. Interactive marketing

8. In marketing, customer _____, lifetime customer value (LCV), or _____ (LTV) and a new concept of 'customer life cycle management' is the present value of the future cash flows attributed to the customer relationship. Use of customer _____ as a marketing metric tends to place greater emphasis on customer service and long-term customer satisfaction, rather than on maximizing short-term sales.

Customer _____ has intuitive appeal as a marketing concept, because in theory it represents exactly how much each customer is worth in monetary terms, and therefore exactly how much a marketing department should be willing to spend to acquire each customer.

   a. Brand infiltration
   b. Sweepstakes
   c. Lifetime value
   d. Value chain

9. _____. People may not recognize the value in offered personalization, such as when firms offer to customize product offers. Many people don't want to receive any such offers, period.
   a. Push
   b. Category Development Index
   c. Bottling lines
   d. Little value placed on potential benefits

10. _____ is an extreme form of product differentiation. Whereas product differentiation tries to differentiate a product from competing ones, personalization tries to make a unique product offering for each customer.

_____ had been most practical in interactive media such as the internet.

   a. Disintermediation
   b. Permission marketing
   c. Social shopping
   d. Personalized marketing

11. A personal and cultural _____ is a relative ethic _____, an assumption upon which implementation can be extrapolated. A _____ system is a set of consistent _____s and measures that is soo not true. A principle _____ is a foundation upon which other _____s and measures of integrity are based.
   a. Package-on-Package
   b. Supreme Court of the United States
   c. Perceptual maps
   d. Value

12. _____ are long-format television commercials, typically five minutes or longer.. _____ are also known as paid programming (or teleshopping in Europe.) Originally, they were a phenomenon that started in the United States where they were typically shown overnight (usually 2:00 a.m. to 6:00 a.m.)

Chapter 19. Managing Personal Communications

a. AMAX
c. ACNielsen
b. ADTECH
d. Infomercials

13. _____ is a method of direct marketing in which a salesperson solicits to prospective customers to buy products or services, either over the phone or through a subsequent face to face or Web conferencing appointment scheduled during the call.

_____ can also include recorded sales pitches programmed to be played over the phone via automatic dialing. _____ has come under fire in recent years, being viewed as an annoyance by many.

a. Joe job
c. Directory Harvest Attack
b. Phishing
d. Telemarketing

14. _____ is a form of communication that typically attempts to persuade potential customers to purchase or to consume more of a particular brand of product or service. 'While now central to the contemporary global economy and the reproduction of global production networks, it is only quite recently that _____ has been more than a marginal influence on patterns of sales and production. The formation of modern _____ was intimately bound up with the emergence of new forms of monopoly capitalism around the end of the 19th and beginning of the 20th century as one element in corporate strategies to create, organize and where possible control markets, especially for mass produced consumer goods.

a. Advertising
c. ACNielsen
b. AMAX
d. ADTECH

15. In the Mediterranean Basin and the Near East, a _____ is a small, separated garden pavilion open on some or all sides. _____s were common in Persia, India, Pakistan, and in the Ottoman Empire from the 13th century onward. Today, there are many _____s in and around the TopkapÄ± Palace in Istanbul, and they are still a relatively common sight in Greece.

a. 6-3-5 Brainwriting
c. 180SearchAssistant
b. Power III
d. Kiosk

16. _____ commonly refers to the electronic retailing / _____ channels industry, which includes such billion dollar companies as Home shoppingN, QVC, eBay, ShopNBC, Buy.com, and Amazon.com. _____ allows consumers to shop for goods while in the privacy of their own home, as opposed to traditional shopping, which requires you to visit brick and mortar stores and shopping malls.

The _____ / electronic retailing industry was created in 1977 when small market radio talk show host Bob Circosta was asked to sell avocado-green-colored can openers live on the air by station owner Bud Paxson when an advertiser traded 112 units of product instead of paying his advertising bill.

a. 180SearchAssistant
c. Home shopping
b. Power III
d. 6-3-5 Brainwriting

17. _____ is the examining of goods or services from retailers with the intent to purchase at that time. _____ is an activity of selection and/or purchase. In some contexts it is considered a leisure activity as well as an economic one.

a. Hawkers
c. Khodebshchik
b. Shopping
d. Discount store

Chapter 19. Managing Personal Communications

18. A _____ or banner ad is a form of advertising on the World Wide Web. This form of online advertising entails embedding an advertisement into a web page. It is intended to attract traffic to a website by linking to the website of the advertiser.
    a. Consumer privacy
    b. Spamvertising
    c. Disintermediation
    d. Web banner

19. _____, also referred to as i-marketing, web marketing, online marketing is the marketing of products or services over the Internet.

The Internet has brought many unique benefits to marketing, one of which being lower costs for the distribution of information and media to a global audience. The interactive nature of _____, both in terms of providing instant response and eliciting responses, is a unique quality of the medium.

   a. AMAX
   b. ADTECH
   c. Internet marketing
   d. ACNielsen

20. A _____ is a plan of action designed to achieve a particular goal.

_____ is different from tactics. In military terms, tactics is concerned with the conduct of an engagement while _____ is concerned with how different engagements are linked.

   a. 180SearchAssistant
   b. Power III
   c. 6-3-5 Brainwriting
   d. Strategy

21. The most important feature of a contract is that one party makes an _____ for an arrangement that another accepts. This can be called a 'concurrence of wills' or 'ad idem' (meeting of the minds) of two or more parties. The concept is somewhat contested.
    a. ACNielsen
    b. ADTECH
    c. AMAX
    d. Offer

22. _____ in economics refers to metrics and measures of output from production processes, per unit of input. Labor _____, for example, is typically measured as a ratio of output per labor-hour, an input. _____ may be conceived of as a metrics of the technical or engineering efficiency of production.
    a. Value engineering
    b. 180SearchAssistant
    c. Power III
    d. Productivity

23. _____ is a form of marketing developed from direct response marketing campaigns conducted in the 1970's and 1980's which emphasizes customer retention and satisfaction, rather than a dominant focus on 'point of sale' transactions.

_____ differs from other forms of marketing in that it recognizes the long term value to the firm of keeping customers, as opposed to direct or 'Intrusion' marketing, which focuses upon acquisition of new clients by targeting majority demographics based upon prospective client lists.

_____ refers to long-term and mutually beneficial arrangement wherein both buyer and seller focus on value enhancement through the certain of more satisfying exchange.This approach attempts to transcend the simple purchase exchange process with customer to make more meaningful and richer contact by providing a more holistic, personalized purchase, and use orn consumption experience to create stronger ties.

- a. Relationship marketing
- b. Global marketing
- c. Diversity marketing
- d. Guerrilla Marketing

24. _____ is a form of targeted advertising for advertisements appearing on websites or other media, such as content displayed in mobile browsers. The advertisements themselves are selected and served by automated systems based on the content displayed to the user.

A _____ system scans the text of a website for keywords and returns advertisements to the webpage based on what the user is viewing.

- a. Contextual advertising
- b. Click fraud
- c. Click-through rate
- d. Multivariate testing

Chapter 20. Introducing New Market Offerings

1. _____ in organizations and public policy is both the organizational process of creating and maintaining a plan; and the psychological process of thinking about the activities required to create a desired goal on some scale. As such, it is a fundamental property of intelligent behavior. This thought process is essential to the creation and refinement of a plan, or integration of it with other plans, that is, it combines forecasting of developments with the preparation of scenarios of how to react to them.

   a. 6-3-5 Brainwriting
   b. Planning
   c. Power III
   d. 180SearchAssistant

2. _____ generally refers to a list of all planned expenses and revenues. It is a plan for saving and spending. A _____ is an important concept in microeconomics, which uses a _____ line to illustrate the trade-offs between two or more goods.

   a. Power III
   b. 180SearchAssistant
   c. 6-3-5 Brainwriting
   d. Budget

3. A _____ is a plan of action designed to achieve a particular goal.

   _____ is different from tactics. In military terms, tactics is concerned with the conduct of an engagement while _____ is concerned with how different engagements are linked.

   a. 180SearchAssistant
   b. 6-3-5 Brainwriting
   c. Power III
   d. Strategy

4. _____ is defined by the American _____ Association as the activity, set of institutions, and processes for creating, communicating, delivering, and exchanging offerings that have value for customers, clients, partners, and society at large. The term developed from the original meaning which referred literally to going to market, as in shopping, or going to a market to sell goods or services.

   _____ practice tends to be seen as a creative industry, which includes advertising, distribution and selling.

   a. Product naming
   b. Marketing myopia
   c. Customer acquisition management
   d. Marketing

5. _____ is the process or cycle of introducing a new product into the market. The actual launch of a new product is the final stage of new product development, and the one where the most money will have to be spent for advertising, sales promotion, and other marketing efforts. In the case of a new consumer packaged good, costs will be at least $ 10 million, but can reach up to $ 200 million.

   a. Commercialization
   b. Sweepstakes
   c. Confusion marketing
   d. Customer Interaction Tracker

6. _____ is a statistical technique used in market research to determine how people value different features that make up an individual product or service.

   The objective of _____ is to determine what combination of a limited number of attributes is most influential on respondent choice or decision making. A controlled set of potential products or services is shown to respondents and by analyzing how they make preferences between these products, the implicit valuation of the individual elements making up the product or service can be determined.

Chapter 20. Introducing New Market Offerings

a. Conjoint analysis
c. Power III
b. Semantic differential
d. Likert scale

7. _____ is the process of transforming information from one format into another. The opposite operation is called decoding.

There are a number of more specific meanings that apply in certain contexts:

- _____ is a basic perceptual process of interpreting incoming stimuli; technically speaking, it is a complex, multi-stage process of converting relatively objective sensory input (e.g., light, sound) into subjectively meaningful experience.
- A content format is a specific _____ format for converting a specific type of data to information.
- Character _____ is a code that pairs a set of natural language characters (such as an alphabet or syllabary) with a set of something else, such as numbers or electrical pulses.
- Text _____ uses a markup language to tag the structure and other features of a text to facilitate processing by computers.
- Semantics _____ of formal language A in formal language B is a method of representing all terms (e.g. programs or descriptions) of language A using language B.
- Electronic _____ transforms a signal into a code optimized for transmission or storage, generally done with a codec.
- Neural _____ is the way in which information is represented in neurons.
- Memory _____ is the process of converting sensations into memories.
- Encryption transforms information for secrecy.

a. Encoding
c. AMAX
b. ACNielsen
d. ADTECH

8. A _____ is a process that can allow an organization to concentrate its limited resources on the greatest opportunities to increase sales and achieve a sustainable competitive advantage. A _____ should be centered around the key concept that customer satisfaction is the main goal.

A _____ is most effective when it is an integral component of corporate strategy, defining how the organization will successfully engage customers, prospects, and competitors in the market arena.

a. Psychographic
c. Societal marketing
b. Marketing strategy
d. Cyberdoc

9. _____ is the set of tasks, knowledge, and techniques required to identify business needs and determine solutions to business problems. Solutions often include a systems development component, but may also consist of process improvement or organizational change. The person who carries out this task is called a business analyst or _____.

a. Marketing management
c. Door-to-door
b. Business analysis
d. Fast moving consumer goods

Chapter 20. Introducing New Market Offerings

10. The break-even point for a product is the point where total revenue received equals the total costs associated with the sale of the product (TR=TC.) A break-even point is typically calculated in order for businesses to determine if it would be profitable to sell a proposed product, as opposed to attempting to modify an existing product instead so it can be made lucrative. _____ can also be used to analyse the potential profitability of an expenditure in a sales-based business.

In _____, margin of safety is how much output or sales level can fall before a business reaches its break-even point (BEP).

   a. Break even analysis
   b. Contribution margin-based pricing
   c. Price skimming
   d. Pay Per Sale

11. In business and engineering, new _____ is the term used to describe the complete process of bringing a new product or service to market. There are two parallel paths involved in the Nproduct development process: one involves the idea generation, product design, and detail engineering; the other involves market research and marketing analysis. Companies typically see new _____ as the first stage in generating and commercializing new products within the overall strategic process of product life cycle management used to maintain or grow their market share.
   a. New product screening
   b. Specification tree
   c. New product development
   d. Product development

12. Proof-of-Principle _____ This type of _____ is used to test some aspect of the intended design without attempting to exactly simulate the visual appearance, choice of materials or intended manufacturing process. Such _____s can be used to 'prove' out a potential design approach such as range of motion, mechanics, sensors, architecture, etc.
   a. 180SearchAssistant
   b. 6-3-5 Brainwriting
   c. Power III
   d. Prototype

13. _____ is a concept that denotes the precise probability of specific eventualities. Technically, the notion of _____ is independent from the notion of value and, as such, eventualities may have both beneficial and adverse consequences. However, in general usage the convention is to focus only on potential negative impact to some characteristic of value that may arise from a future event.
   a. 180SearchAssistant
   b. 6-3-5 Brainwriting
   c. Power III
   d. Risk

14. A _____, in the field of business and marketing, is a geographic region or demographic group used to gauge the viability of a product or service in the mass market prior to a wide scale roll-out. The criteria used to judge the acceptability of a _____ region or group include:

   1. a population that is demographically similar to the proposed target market; and
   2. relative isolation from densely populated media markets so that advertising to the test audience can be efficient and economical.

The _____ ideally aims to duplicate 'everything' - promotion and distribution as well as `product' - on a smaller scale. The technique replicates, typically in one area, what is planned to occur in a national launch; and the results are very carefully monitored, so that they can be extrapolated to projected national results. The `area' may be any one of the following:

- Television area
- Test town
- Residential neighborhood
- Test site

A number of decisions have to be taken about any _____:

- Which _____?
- What is to be tested?
- How long a test?
- What are the success criteria?

The simple go or no-go decision, together with the related reduction of risk, is normally the main justification for the expense of _____s. At the same time, however, such _____s can be used to test specific elements of a new product's marketing mix; possibly the version of the product itself, the promotional message and media spend, the distribution channels and the price.

a. 180SearchAssistant
c. Preadolescence
b. Power III
d. Test market

15. _____ is a broad label that refers to any individuals or households that use goods and services generated within the economy. The concept of a _____ is used in different contexts, so that the usage and significance of the term may vary.

A _____ is a person who uses any product or service.

a. 6-3-5 Brainwriting
c. Consumer
b. Power III
d. 180SearchAssistant

16. _____ is the process by which a new idea or new product is accepted by the market. The rate of _____ is the speed that the new idea spreads from one consumer to the next. Adoption is similar to _____ except that it deals with the psychological processes an individual goes through, rather than an aggregate market process.

a. Perceptual maps
c. Kano model
b. Diffusion
d. Market development

17. In probability theory, a branch of mathematics, a _____ is a solution to a stochastic differential equation. It is a continuous-time Markov process with continuous sample paths.

A sample path of a _____ mimics the trajectory of a molecule, which is embedded in a flowing fluid and at the same time subjected to random displacements due to collisions with other molecules, i.e. Brownian motion.

a. 180SearchAssistant
b. Power III
c. 6-3-5 Brainwriting
d. Diffusion process

Chapter 21. Tapping into Global Markets

1. _____ is a measure of the strength of a brand, product, service relative to competitive offerings. There is often a geographic element to the competitive landscape. In defining _____, you must see to what extent a product, brand, or firm controls a product category in a given geographic area.
   a. Market system
   b. Discretionary spending
   c. Productivity
   d. Market dominance

2. An _____ is the manufacturing of a good or service within a category. Although _____ is a broad term for any kind of economic production, in economics and urban planning _____ is a synonym for the secondary sector, which is a type of economic activity involved in the manufacturing of raw materials into goods and products.

   There are four key industrial economic sectors: the primary sector, largely raw material extraction industries such as mining and farming; the secondary sector, involving refining, construction, and manufacturing; the tertiary sector, which deals with services (such as law and medicine) and distribution of manufactured goods; and the quaternary sector, a relatively new type of knowledge _____ focusing on technological research, design and development such as computer programming, and biochemistry.

   a. AMAX
   b. ADTECH
   c. ACNielsen
   d. Industry

3. _____ is defined by the American _____ Association as the activity, set of institutions, and processes for creating, communicating, delivering, and exchanging offerings that have value for customers, clients, partners, and society at large. The term developed from the original meaning which referred literally to going to market, as in shopping, or going to a market to sell goods or services.

   _____ practice tends to be seen as a creative industry, which includes advertising, distribution and selling.

   a. Marketing
   b. Product naming
   c. Customer acquisition management
   d. Marketing myopia

4. _____s is the social science that studies the production, distribution, and consumption of goods and services. The term _____s comes from the Ancient Greek oá¼°κονομῖα from oá¼¶κος (oikos, 'house') + vΐŒμος (nomos, 'custom' or 'law'), hence 'rules of the house(hold)'. Current _____ models developed out of the broader field of political economy in the late 19th century, owing to a desire to use an empirical approach more akin to the physical sciences.
   a. ACNielsen
   b. Economic
   c. ADTECH
   d. Industrial organization

5. The _____ is an economic and political union of 27 member states, located primarily in Europe. It was established by the Treaty of Maastricht on 1 November 1993 upon the foundations of the pre-existing European Economic Community. With almost 500 million citizens, the _____ combined generates an estimated 30% share (US$16.8 trillion in 2007) of the nominal gross world product.
   a. ADTECH
   b. ACNielsen
   c. Eurozone
   d. European Union

Chapter 21. Tapping into Global Markets

6. A _____ or export processing zone (EPZ) is one or more special areas of a country where some normal trade barriers such as tariffs and quotas are eliminated and bureaucratic requirements are lowered in hopes of attracting new business and foreign investments. It is a a region where a group of countries has agreed to reduce or eliminate trade barriers. They can be defined as labor intensive manufacturing centers that involve the import of raw materials or components and the export of factory products.

   a. Green market
   b. Customs union
   c. Competitive
   d. Free Trade Zone

7. In economics, an _____ is any good or commodity, transported from one country to another country in a legitimate fashion, typically for use in trade. _____ goods or services are provided to foreign consumers by domestic producers. _____ is an important part of international trade.

   a. AMAX
   b. ADTECH
   c. ACNielsen
   d. Export

8. A _____ is a plan of action designed to achieve a particular goal.

   _____ is different from tactics. In military terms, tactics is concerned with the conduct of an engagement while _____ is concerned with how different engagements are linked.

   a. 6-3-5 Brainwriting
   b. Strategy
   c. Power III
   d. 180SearchAssistant

9. A _____ is a firm that manufactures components or products for another 'hiring' firm. Many industries utilize this process, especially the aerospace, defense, computer, semiconductor, energy, medical, food manufacturing, personal care, and automotive fields. Some types of contract manufacturing include CNC machining, complex assembly, aluminum die casting, grinding, broaching, gears, and forging.

   a. 180SearchAssistant
   b. Productivity
   c. Power III
   d. Contract manufacturer

10. _____ refers to the methods of practicing and using another person's philosophy of business. The franchisor grants the independent operator the right to distribute its products, techniques, and trademarks for a percentage of gross monthly sales and a royalty fee. Various tangibles and intangibles such as national or international advertising, training, and other support services are commonly made available by the franchisor.

    a. Franchising
    b. Power III
    c. 180SearchAssistant
    d. Franchise fee

11. A _____ is an entity formed between two or more parties to undertake economic activity together. The parties agree to create a new entity by both contributing equity, and they then share in the revenues, expenses, and control of the enterprise. The venture can be for one specific project only, or a continuing business relationship such as the Fuji Xerox _____.

    a. Joint venture
    b. Gripe site
    c. Trademark attorney
    d. Consumer protection

12. The verb _____ or grant _____ means to give permission. The noun _____ refers to that permission as well as to the document memorializing that permission. _____ may be granted by a party to another party as an element of an agreement between those parties.

a. 180SearchAssistant
c. Power III
b. 6-3-5 Brainwriting
d. License

13. Foreign _____ in its classic form is defined as a company from one country making a physical investment into building a factory in another country. It is the establishment of an enterprise by a foreigner. Its definition can be extended to include investments made to acquire lasting interest in enterprises operating outside of the economy of the investor.
   a. Fountain Fresh International
   b. Brash Brands
   c. VideoJug
   d. Direct investment

14. The _____ was the outcome of the failure of negotiating governments to create the International Trade Organization (ITO.) GATT was formed in 1947 and lasted until 1994, when it was replaced by the World Trade Organization. The Bretton Woods Conference had introduced the idea for an organization to regulate trade as part of a larger plan for economic recovery after World War II.
   a. General Agreement on Trade in Services
   b. Power III
   c. General Agreement on Tariffs and Trade
   d. Trade pact

15. A _____ is a tax imposed on goods when they are moved across a political boundary. They are usually associated with protectionism, the economic policy of restraining trade between nations. For political reasons, _____ s are usually imposed on imported goods, although they may also be imposed on exported goods.
   a. Fiscal policy
   b. Power III
   c. Tariff
   d. Monetary policy

16. In economics, '_____' can refer to any kind of predatory pricing. However, the word is now generally used only in the context of international trade law, where _____ is defined as the act of a manufacturer in one country exporting a product to another country at a price which is either below the price it charges in its home market or is below its costs of production. The term has a negative connotation, but advocates of free markets see '_____' as beneficial for consumers and believe that protectionism to prevent it would have net negative consequences.
   a. Sample sales
   b. Gold Key Matching Service
   c. Hawkers
   d. Dumping

17. A grey market or _____ is the trade of a commodity through distribution channels which, while legal, are unofficial, unauthorized, or unintended by the original manufacturer. In contrast, a black market is the trade of goods and services that are illegal in themselves and/or distributed through illegal channels, such as the selling of stolen goods or illegal items such as heroin or unregistered handguns.

The two main types of grey market are imported manufactured goods that would be normally unavailable or more expensive in a certain country and unissued securities that are not yet traded in official markets.

   a. Customs union
   b. Gray market
   c. Green market
   d. Zone pricing

18. _____ in economics and business is the result of an exchange and from that trade we assign a numerical monetary value to a good, service or asset. If I trade 4 apples for an orange, the _____ of an orange is 4 - apples. Inversely, the _____ of an apple is 1/4 oranges.

a. Contribution margin-based pricing
b. Discounts and allowances
c. Pricing
d. Price

19. _____ is a technique used in propaganda and advertising. Also known as association, this is a technique of projecting positive or negative qualities (praise or blame) of a person, entity, object, or value (an individual, group, organization, nation, patriotism, etc.) to another in order to make the second more acceptable or to discredit it.

a. Sexism,
b. Micro ads
c. Transfer
d. Supplier

20. _____ is one of the four elements of marketing mix. An organization or set of organizations (go-betweens) involved in the process of making a product or service available for use or consumption by a consumer or business user.

The other three parts of the marketing mix are product, pricing, and promotion.

a. Comparison-Shopping agent
b. Japan Advertising Photographers' Association
c. Better Living Through Chemistry
d. Distribution

21. A _____ is a collection of symbols, experiences and associations connected with a product, a service, a person or any other artifact or entity.

_____s have become increasingly important components of culture and the economy, now being described as 'cultural accessories and personal philosophies'.

Some people distinguish the psychological aspect of a _____ from the experiential aspect.

a. Brand equity
b. Brandable software
c. Brand
d. Store brand

Chapter 22. Managing a Holistic Marketing Organization

1. _____ is defined by the American _____ Association as the activity, set of institutions, and processes for creating, communicating, delivering, and exchanging offerings that have value for customers, clients, partners, and society at large. The term developed from the original meaning which referred literally to going to market, as in shopping, or going to a market to sell goods or services.

_____ practice tends to be seen as a creative industry, which includes advertising, distribution and selling.

   a. Product naming
   b. Marketing myopia
   c. Customer acquisition management
   d. Marketing

2. _____ is an ongoing process that occurs strictly within a company or organization whereby the functional process aligns, motivates and empowers employees at all management levels to consistently deliver a satisfying customer experience. According to Burkitt and Zealley, 'the challenge for _____ is not only to get the right messages across, but to embed them in such a way that they both change and reinforce employee behaviour'.
   a. ACNielsen
   b. Internal marketing
   c. AMAX
   d. ADTECH

3. _____ is the study of the Earth and its lands, features, inhabitants, and phenomena. A literal translation would be 'to describe or write about the Earth'. The first person to use the word '_____' was Eratosthenes .
   a. Geography
   b. 6-3-5 Brainwriting
   c. 180SearchAssistant
   d. Power III

4. _____ is the process or cycle of introducing a new product into the market. The actual launch of a new product is the final stage of new product development, and the one where the most money will have to be spent for advertising, sales promotion, and other marketing efforts. In the case of a new consumer packaged good, costs will be at least $ 10 million, but can reach up to $ 200 million.
   a. Confusion marketing
   b. Customer Interaction Tracker
   c. Sweepstakes
   d. Commercialization

5. _____ is the practice of individuals including commercial businesses, governments and institutions, facilitating the sale of their products or services to other companies or organizations that in turn resell them, use them as components in products or services they offer _____ is also called business-to-_____ for short. (Note that while marketing to government entities shares some of the same dynamics of organizational marketing, B2G Marketing is meaningfully different.)
   a. Business marketing
   b. Mass marketing
   c. Law of disruption
   d. Disruptive technology

6. _____ refers to a business or organization attempting to acquire goods or services to accomplish the goals of the enterprise. Though there are several organizations that attempt to set standards in the _____ process, processes can vary greatly between organizations. Typically the word '_____' is not used interchangeably with the word 'procurement', since procurement typically includes Expediting, Supplier Quality, and Traffic and Logistics (T'L) in addition to _____.
   a. Supply network
   b. Supply chain
   c. Drop shipping
   d. Purchasing

Chapter 22. Managing a Holistic Marketing Organization

7. _____ also known as corporate responsibility, corporate citizenship, responsible business, sustainable responsible business and corporate social performance' is a form of corporate self-regulation integrated into a business model. Ideally, _____ policy would function as a built-in, self-regulating mechanism whereby business would monitor and ensure their adherence to law, ethical standards, and international norms. Business would embrace responsibility for the impact of their activities on the environment, consumers, employees, communities, stakeholders and all other members of the public sphere.
    a. 6-3-5 Brainwriting
    b. 180SearchAssistant
    c. Corporate social responsibility
    d. Power III

8. _____ refers to a type of marketing involving the cooperative efforts of a 'for profit' business and a non-profit organization for mutual benefit. The term is sometimes used more broadly and generally to refer to any type of marketing effort for social and other charitable causes, including in-house marketing efforts by non-profit organizations. Cause marketing differs from corporate giving (philanthropy) as the latter generally involves a specific donation that is tax deductible, while cause marketing is a marketing relationship generally not based on a donation.
    a. Diversity marketing
    b. Digital marketing
    c. Global marketing
    d. Cause-related marketing

9. The _____ concept is an enlightened marketing concept that holds that a company should make good marketing decisions by considering consumers' wants, the company's requirements, and society's long-term interests. It is closely linked with the principles of corporate social responsibility and of sustainable development.

    The concept has an emphasis on social responsibility and suggests that for a company to only focus on exchange relationship with customers might not be suitable in order to sustain long term success.

    a. Marketing
    b. Business-to-business
    c. Customer franchise
    d. Societal marketing

10. _____ is the systematic application of marketing along with other concepts and techniques to achieve specific behavioral goals for a social good. _____ can be applied to promote, for example, merit goods, make the society avoid demerit goods and thus to promote that considers society's well being as a whole. This may include asking people not to smoke in public areas, for example, ask them to use seat belts, prompting to make them follow speed limits.
    a. Psychographic
    b. Market development
    c. Marketing strategy
    d. Social marketing

11. _____ is the realization of an application idea, model, design, specification, standard, algorithm an _____ is a realization of a technical specification or algorithm as a program, software component, or other computer system. Many _____s may exist for a given specification or standard.
    a. AMAX
    b. ADTECH
    c. Implementation
    d. ACNielsen

12. _____ is systematic determination of merit, worth, and significance of something or someone using criteria against a set of standards. _____ often is used to characterize and appraise subjects of interest in a wide range of human enterprises, including the arts, criminal justice, foundations and non-profit organizations, government, health care, and other human services.

Depending on the topic of interest, there are professional groups which look to the quality and rigor of the _____ process.

a. ADTECH
b. Evaluation
c. AMAX
d. ACNielsen

13. _____ is a form of communication that typically attempts to persuade potential customers to purchase or to consume more of a particular brand of product or service. 'While now central to the contemporary global economy and the reproduction of global production networks, it is only quite recently that _____ has been more than a marginal influence on patterns of sales and production. The formation of modern _____ was intimately bound up with the emergence of new forms of monopoly capitalism around the end of the 19th century and beginning of the 20th century as one element in corporate strategies to create, organize and where possible control markets, especially for mass produced consumer goods.

a. Advertising
b. ACNielsen
c. AMAX
d. ADTECH

14. _____ is one of the four elements of marketing mix. An organization or set of organizations (go-betweens) involved in the process of making a product or service available for use or consumption by a consumer or business user.

The other three parts of the marketing mix are product, pricing, and promotion.

a. Better Living Through Chemistry
b. Distribution
c. Japan Advertising Photographers' Association
d. Comparison-Shopping agent

15. _____ is one of the four aspects of promotional mix. (The other three parts of the promotional mix are advertising, personal selling, and publicity/public relations.) Media and non-media marketing communication are employed for a pre-determined, limited time to increase consumer demand, stimulate market demand or improve product availability.

a. Marketing communication
b. Sales promotion
c. Merchandise
d. New Media Strategies

16. _____ involves disseminating information about a product, product line, brand, or company. It is one of the four key aspects of the marketing mix. (The other three elements are product marketing, pricing, and distribution). P>_____ is generally sub-divided into two parts:

- Above the line _____: Promotion in the media (e.g. TV, radio, newspapers, Internet and Mobile Phones) in which the advertiser pays an advertising agency to place the ad
- Below the line _____: All other _____. Much of this is intended to be subtle enough for the consumer to be unaware that _____ is taking place. E.g. sponsorship, product placement, endorsements, sales _____, merchandising, direct mail, personal selling, public relations, trade shows

a. Davie Brown Index
b. Bottling lines
c. Promotion
d. Cashmere Agency

17. The general definition of an _____ is an evaluation of a person, organization, system, process, project or product. _____s are performed to ascertain the validity and reliability of information; also to provide an assessment of a system's internal control. The goal of an _____ is to express an opinion on the person/organization/system (etc) in question, under evaluation based on work done on a test basis.
   a. AMAX   b. ACNielsen
   c. ADTECH   d. Audit

ANSWER KEY

Chapter 1
1. d   2. d   3. d   4. d   5. d   6. d   7. b   8. a   9. d   10. c
11. d   12. a   13. c   14. b   15. c   16. d   17. c   18. a   19. d   20. d
21. d   22. a   23. d   24. d   25. c   26. b   27. b   28. b   29. a   30. b
31. c   32. d   33. d   34. c   35. d   36. d   37. b   38. b

Chapter 2
1. d   2. d   3. c   4. b   5. c   6. b   7. d   8. a   9. d   10. d
11. b   12. c   13. c   14. a   15. a   16. c   17. d   18. b   19. c   20. c
21. a   22. b   23. d   24. d   25. d   26. d   27. c   28. b   29. d   30. d
31. d   32. d   33. d

Chapter 3
1. b   2. a   3. d   4. d   5. b   6. d   7. b   8. c   9. d   10. d
11. a   12. d   13. b   14. a   15. b   16. d   17. c   18. c   19. d   20. a

Chapter 4
1. d   2. d   3. a   4. a   5. c   6. a   7. a   8. d   9. d   10. b
11. d   12. a   13. d   14. a   15. b   16. d   17. d   18. b   19. b   20. a
21. a   22. a   23. a   24. a   25. d   26. d   27. d   28. d   29. d   30. b
31. d   32. d   33. d   34. c   35. a   36. b   37. c

Chapter 5
1. b   2. d   3. b   4. a   5. d   6. d   7. a   8. b   9. d   10. d
11. b   12. d   13. a   14. a   15. b   16. c   17. b   18. d   19. d   20. b
21. c   22. c   23. d   24. d   25. d   26. d   27. d   28. d   29. c

Chapter 6
1. a   2. d   3. b   4. d   5. d   6. d   7. a   8. d   9. c   10. a
11. d   12. d   13. d   14. d   15. d   16. d   17. d   18. d   19. c   20. b
21. a   22. b   23. d   24. d   25. d   26. a   27. d   28. a   29. d

Chapter 7
1. d   2. d   3. d   4. d   5. b   6. d   7. d   8. a   9. a   10. b
11. b   12. b   13. a   14. d   15. d   16. c   17. d

Chapter 8
1. d   2. d   3. c   4. b   5. b   6. d   7. b   8. a   9. b   10. a
11. b   12. d   13. d   14. d   15. a   16. d   17. d   18. a   19. b   20. a
21. b   22. b   23. a   24. a   25. d

Chapter 9
1. d   2. a   3. b   4. d   5. d   6. b   7. d   8. c   9. c   10. c
11. b   12. d   13. d   14. b   15. d   16. d   17. a   18. c   19. b   20. d
21. d

ANSWER KEY

Chapter 10
1. d   2. d   3. c   4. a   5. d   6. a   7. b   8. d   9. c   10. d
11. d   12. b   13. d   14. a   15. d   16. c

Chapter 11
1. b   2. c   3. d   4. d   5. c   6. d   7. d   8. d   9. c   10. d
11. d   12. b   13. d   14. b

Chapter 12
1. a   2. a   3. d   4. d   5. b   6. d   7. d   8. d   9. d   10. d
11. d   12. b   13. d   14. d   15. d

Chapter 13
1. d   2. a   3. d   4. a   5. b   6. a   7. a   8. a   9. d   10. d
11. b   12. d   13. a   14. d   15. d   16. d   17. a

Chapter 14
1. b   2. d   3. b   4. a   5. d   6. d   7. d   8. c   9. d   10. c
11. d   12. c   13. d   14. d   15. b   16. b   17. c   18. d   19. d   20. c
21. d   22. b   23. d

Chapter 15
1. a   2. a   3. a   4. c   5. d   6. c   7. d   8. d   9. d   10. d
11. a   12. b   13. b   14. a   15. d

Chapter 16
1. b   2. c   3. d   4. c   5. a   6. c   7. a   8. d   9. c   10. d
11. d   12. c   13. d   14. d   15. c   16. a   17. d   18. a   19. b   20. d

Chapter 17
1. d   2. b   3. d   4. d   5. d   6. d   7. c   8. d   9. b   10. b
11. a   12. a   13. c   14. a   15. d   16. a   17. d   18. a   19. b

Chapter 18
1. b   2. d   3. d   4. a   5. d   6. d   7. d   8. d   9. d   10. c
11. d   12. b   13. a   14. d   15. d   16. d   17. d   18. b   19. a   20. d

Chapter 19
1. c   2. b   3. d   4. c   5. d   6. b   7. d   8. c   9. d   10. d
11. d   12. d   13. d   14. a   15. d   16. c   17. b   18. d   19. c   20. d
21. d   22. d   23. a   24. a

Chapter 20
1. b	2. d	3. d	4. d	5. a	6. a	7. a	8. b	9. b	10. a
11. d	12. d	13. d	14. d	15. c	16. b	17. d			

Chapter 21
1. d	2. d	3. a	4. b	5. d	6. d	7. d	8. b	9. d	10. a
11. a	12. d	13. d	14. c	15. c	16. d	17. b	18. d	19. c	20. d
21. c									

Chapter 22
1. d	2. b	3. a	4. d	5. a	6. d	7. c	8. d	9. d	10. d
11. c	12. b	13. a	14. b	15. b	16. c	17. d			

www.ingramcontent.com/pod-product-compliance
Lightning Source LLC
Chambersburg PA
CBHW082051230426
43670CB00016B/2859